DOWN ON THE KORNER

DOWN ON THE KORNER
Ralph Kiner and *Kiner's Korner*

MARK ROSENMAN AND HOWIE KARPIN

Foreword by
Tim McCarver

Carrel Books may be purchased in bulk at special discounts for sales promotion, corporate gifts, fund-raising, or educational purposes. Special editions can also be created to specifications. For details, contact the Special Sales Department, Carrel Books, 307 West 36th Street, 11th Floor, New York, NY 10018, or carrelbooks@skyhorsepublishing.com.

Carrel Books® is a registered trademark of Skyhorse Publishing, Inc.®, a Delaware corporation.

Visit our website at www.carrelbooks.com.

10 9 8 7 6 5 4 3 2 1

Library of Congress Cataloging-in-Publication Data is available on file.

Cover design by Tom Lau
Cover photo credit: Associated Press

ISBN: 978-1-63144-042-7
Ebook ISBN: 978-1-63144-043-4

Printed in the United States of America

DEDICATION

This book is dedicated to the Holy Trinity of New York Mets Broadcasters Bob Murphy, Lindsey Nelson, and the subject of *Down on the Korner*, Ralph Kiner. Thank you for providing the soundtrack of the summers of our lives. Summers just aren't the same since you are gone . . .

CONTENTS

FOREWORD

BY TIM McCARVER

EVEN BEFORE I had the privilege of sitting next to Ralph Kiner for sixteen years as his partner on New York Mets' telecasts, I sat next to him as his guest on *Kiner's Korner* as a player.

Those were more mercenary days, when Ralph used to whip out a fifty dollar bill for being on his postgame show at Shea Stadium. Boy, have things changed!

Our time together (from 1983 to 1998) coincided with the development of a 1986 Mets World Series Championship that captivated New York City. They were a team that owned the Apple—to its core. For at least ten years, the Yankees were a footnote.

I was hired originally to try to extract from Ralph his deep-seated knowledge of the game, and another of his strengths, his storytelling ability.

Ralph never let facts get in the way of a good story, and as the years went by, it became apparent that while the tales may not always have been factual, they had his charm that added such a fiber of goodness to his stories. Also, Ralph was living these stories once again, with the mirth and merriment of his earlier experiences.

There is a distinction here. If a storyteller is of a contemporary ilk, the listener, for the most part, expects the facts to be right. Ralph's tales were from World War II to the mid-to-late fifties, so few were around to confirm them!

So "Kiner Talk," or "Kinerisms," originated.

His "malaprops" were part of his charm, taking on a warmth seldom matched or enjoyed.

One night, Ralph introduced me on the telecast as "Tim McArthur" and I reminded him of it later on in the telecast. At this point, Ralph used his baseball knowledge and his quick wit to make a smooth transition to a commercial break in our telecast.

I said "Ralph, earlier in the game you mistakenly called me 'MacArthur,'" and we talked about General [Douglas] MacArthur, "and one of General MacArthur's lines was 'Chance favors the prepared man' and obviously the Mets weren't prepared tonight." Ralph turned toward the camera and said "MacArthur also said, 'I shall return,' and we'll be right back right after this.'"

However, my very favorite "you can't make this up" story with Ralph also happened in the broadcast booth one otherwise uneventful sultry summer night.

As Ralph and I were going over our notes and preparing for a game, a gentleman came in, sat down, and started carrying on this conversation as though we were the best of friends. Meanwhile, I am struggling and racking my brain with the one thought: "Who is this guy?" Mercifully, after five minutes, he leaves and I turn to my partner and say, "Man, I hate that—talking to someone for five minutes, with that phony smile, and thinking all the time, 'Just give me a clue as to who you are." Ralph looks over and says, "You know what I do in those situations? I simply say 'There he is!' (Keep in mind that on the air, Ralph has referred to me as Ted, Jim, Jed, Terry, MacArthur, McCarthy, and Macgarver.) So I say, "Partner, that's an old way of getting out of it. For me, that just doesn't cut it." So, we do the game and the next night, Ralph is working on his notes. As I saunter into the booth, he looks up, and you guessed it, Ralph says, "There he is!" A partner with whom I had worked for years, in just 24 hours, has forgotten my name . . . again!

The camaraderie between us was special. He was a friend, brother, and father.

Of course, his past *Kiner's Korner* shows are highlighted in the book with guests such as Willie Mays, Casey Stengel, Stan Musial, Keith Hernandez, and 'Choo Choo' Coleman.

Ralph Kiner was revered not only for what he would say, but more importantly, for how he would say it.

And I had such reverence for his irreverence.

With warmth and sincerity,
Ted, Jim, Jed, Terry, MacArthur, McCarthy, Macgarver . . . and Tim

1

"The Mets hired me because they looked at my background with the Pirates and saw that I had losing experience."

FOR MOST OF his ten-year career, outfielder Ralph Kiner was one of the most feared home run hitters in the National League. From 1946 to 1955, the 6'2" slugger hit 369 career home runs. Three hundred one of those long balls came during his first eight years with the Pittsburgh Pirates, a perennial loser in those days.

Kiner was a powerful right-handed hitter who took advantage of the left field dimensions at Forbes Field. When the ballpark opened in 1909, it was 365 feet down the left field line, but a significant addition would lead to an alteration of the ballpark's dimensions in left field.

In January of 1947, the Pirates purchased the contract of future Hall of Famer and right handed power hitter Hank Greenberg from the Detroit Tigers. In order to take full advantage of Greenberg's power, the left field wall was moved in thirty feet and the left center field gap was reduced from 406 to 376 feet. The area, which also housed the Pirates bullpen, became known as "Greenberg's Gardens."

Kiner met Greenberg (the man he would call "the single biggest influence of my adult life") in spring training. "I idolized him when I was growing up in Los Angeles," Kiner said. On the first day, Greenberg

Hank Greenberg taught Ralph that "hard
work was the way to succeed."
(Harris & Ewing, via Wikimedia Commons)

suggested they take extra batting practice. Kiner heeded his idol's advice,
believing that "hard work was the way to succeed." The two sluggers
became fast friends and were roommates on road trips.

After hitting twenty-three home runs in his rookie season, Kiner
started slowly in 1947 and Pirates manager Billy Herman was thinking of
sending him down to the minors. Greenberg intervened and convinced
the owner, Frank McKinney to keep the twenty-four-year old with the
big club and it turned out to be the right move.

Kiner went on to hit fifty-one home runs and tie for the league lead.
Two years later, the right-handed slugger would hit fifty-four home runs
and bat .310. Kiner finished fourth in the voting in 1949 for the National
League's Most Valuable Player award.

Legend had it that local sportswriters reportedly renamed "Greenberg's
Gardens" with the moniker "Kiner's Korner." That was disputed in an
article that was written by sportscaster and journalist Eddie Lucas when
he interviewed Kiner for the *Jersey Journal* in April 2012.[1] According
to the article, Kiner said the "credit goes to the fans at Pittsburgh's old
Forbes Field, who first named the left field area in that park."

Kiner credits the Forbes Field fans for
"Kiners Korner"
(Bowman, via Wikimedia Commons)

While Kiner played in Pittsburgh, the famous crooner and actor Bing Crosby was a part owner of the club. That connection allowed Kiner to rub elbows with Hollywood's elite and date some famous actresses like Elizabeth Taylor, Ava Gardner, Jane Russell, Marilyn Monroe, and Janet Leigh.

In the 1950s, the California native moved to Palm Springs and married tennis star Nancy Chaffe. He played golf with celebrities like Frank Sinatra, Jack Benny, and Bob Hope, while Lucille Ball and Desi Arnaz were the Kiners' neighbors, so there was no lack of star power.

Kiner was traded to the Chicago Cubs in June 1953 and was eventually sent to the Cleveland Indians. After playing the 1955 season with Cleveland, a bad back forced Kiner into early retirement. He was thirty-two years old.

In 1956, Kiner accepted a job as the General Manager of the San Diego Padres, the Cleveland Indians' AAA affiliate. As a money-saving measure, Kiner began broadcasting the games himself.

Kiner's broadcasting career took another step forward in 1960 when he conducted interviews at the Bing Crosby Golf Tournament. He also did post-game interviews for Pirates games.

Kiner's responsibilities included a postgame show.
(Photo courtesy of Gene Samuels)

In 1961, he got his first big break, thanks to an old friend. Greenberg, then the General Manager of the Chicago White Sox, hired Kiner to be part of the broadcast team.

The next year, Kiner was hired to broadcast games for the expansion New York Mets. The former Pirate reportedly reacted to his hiring with this line which gave an early insight into his personality and wit. Kiner said, "The Mets hired me because they looked at my background with the Pirates and saw that I had losing experience."

One of his responsibilities included a postgame show where he would interview the "star of the game."

"The show was broadcast way before you could see all these players every night," said *New York Daily News* Sports Media Columnist Bob Raissman.

"You could see a Willie Mays there who obviously was a superstar and see him actually talking to Ralph Kiner. It was before these interview shows, these one-on-one interviews. You look back on it, it was kind of a rarity."

Like the Mets, *Kiner's Korner* began in 1962 and the show's title seemed like a perfect choice, since it harkened back to Kiner's playing career.

"The Flag of Victory Polka" by Ira Ironstrings was chosen as the show's official theme song. In the later years of the show, the theme was changed once again, but most fans consider "The Flag of Victory Polka" as the official theme song.

"I believe we did change it at one time," said Jeff Mitchell, the former producer and director of Mets broadcasts in the 1980s that included *Kiner's Korner*. It was one of those things we were thinking about changing it a little bit. We did, I don't know if we continued on or we changed back. I know we did change it at one time to get a different feel for the show."

Each episode of *Kiner's Korner* would usually last about fifteen minutes, but there were many times that it wasn't long enough. "We did a show one time with Casey Stengel," said Emmy-Award winning director Bill Webb, who directed the show and Mets game telecasts from 1979 to 1987. "Ralph Kiner asked one question and Casey would never stop talking so what happened was, we had to go to 'black,' fade audio, and

Casey Stengel
(Topps trading cards used courtesy of the Topps Company, Inc.)

come up on commercial. Then, we'd do the same thing coming out of commercial. We'd come up on 'black' and Casey was still talking. We did that three times."

From 1962 to 1965, Joe Gallagher was the first producer of *Kiner's Korner*. In lieu of using a professional announcer, it was decided that Kiner would host the show.

Kiner's Korner was known for being a post-game show, but, in the early years, there was a show before the game. "We did a pre-game show for every home game," Gallagher said. "It started in '62, the first year of the team. At that time, I had been working as a producer for CBS Sports. When Rheingold beer changed agencies, they moved to the J. Walter Thompson agency. The man who was in charge of putting together the broadcast team was CEO Norman Strouse, and he recruited me to be the producer. Ralph had already been hired through the team. The head of broadcast operations at J. Walter Thompson was Dan Seymour, (who had experience as a radio announcer) and he recruited Lindsey Nelson and Bob Murphy."

Newsday Sports Media Columnist Neil Best said the lack of interaction with the athletes and personalities of that time helped the show gain a following. "If you tried to put that on television now, obviously you'd be laughed off because the production values were so low and the whole thing was so, sort of clunky, but at the time, it was invaluable because that was all we had," Best said. "Even if you watched the games back in that era you weren't getting that many close-ups. [*Kiner's Korner*] was the only time you got to hear these players speak."

"The thing I always think about," Raissman said, "[was that] it was really natural. Compared to what goes on today, [the show] wasn't over-produced. It was basically Ralph and these guys. He could come up with some strange questions. He would be getting funny answers. It was humorous. You learned a little bit about baseball. The thing about it is how long it lasted."

Gallagher said he and Ralph were not on the same page about the title.

"When we started, Ralph wanted to use the 'K' on both, of course Kiner with a 'K'. I said no, corner is with a 'C.'

At least the four years that I produced the show, we spelled [corner] with a 'C.' It was Ralph's wish at the beginning to use a 'K,' but he didn't make an issue of it. He said, 'Let's start with the right way.' Ralph was not a guy to quibble over little things so it was *Kiner's Korner* but the 'Korner' was spelled with a 'C.' Somewhere along the line, they changed it," Gallagher said.

The show's title aside, Gallagher and Kiner were on the same page when it came to the guests. "I would consult with Ralph," said Gallagher. "We would talk and I would tell him maybe what I had in mind for the next day for a pre-game show. It usually was sort of obvious or there was kind of an overall plan to it. Ralph was an easy guy to work with, he was a very pleasant man."

"On the postgame show it was more or less usually obvious, at least who the 'star of the game' was. We always went with who we thought was the 'star of the game,' and that meant most of the time we had visiting players on."

"Usually I would send somebody out to the field to get the player because I was supervising what was going on on TV and helping set up the postgame show", Gallagher said. "I would consult with Ralph and say, 'Should we have [Red] Schoendienst on or Ken Boyer on?' and Ralph usually made the decisions."

In 1973, Mitchell was a production assistant and was responsible for bringing guests on the show. In the fifth inning of Game Three of the National League Championship Series, Cincinnati's Pete Rose slid hard into Mets shortstop Bud Harrelson in an attempt to break up the double play.

Afterwards, the two began fighting out at second base, with the burly Rose getting the better of the slender Harrelson. Order was restored on the field and the Mets went on to win the game 9–2 but not before the fans vented their anger towards the Reds star.

When Rose took his position in left field, the fans disrupted the game by throwing garbage at him. Reds manager Sparky Anderson took the team off the field as a safety precaution, which riled the fans even more. It was not until Mets manager Yogi Berra, Willie Mays, Tom Seaver, Cleon Jones, and Rusty Staub walked out to appeal to the fans to calm down and avoid a forfeit, that play was able to resume.

Rose was in the "eye of the hurricane" as far as the controversy was concerned so Kiner wanted him on the show. "Ralph came into in the control room, smoking a cigar. In those days, you could smoke a cigar anywhere," Mitchell said. "He came down about the eighth inning or so. On that day, he said 'Jeff, could you go down and get Pete Rose out of the visitors clubhouse.' I said 'ok.'"

Mitchell was in a bit of a quandary, as he didn't want to disappoint Kiner.

"Rose had just gotten into a fight with (Bud) Harrelson at second base. So I go down to the clubhouse, I said to myself, 'How am I gonna get Rose', and 'where is he?' I was twenty-one years old."

Mitchell found a way and scored a coup for *Kiner's Korner*. "I saw this big crowd around this one locker. 'That's gotta be Pete.' I see Pete sittin' down on a stool with all the reporters around asking him questions. I gotta get him on the show. I stand up on a stool and yelled out, 'Hey Pete, you wanna go on *Kiner's Korner*?' He goes 'yeah.' I reach in and grab him, pull him out, and take him down to the set. It was pretty amazing that we got him on the show," said Mitchell.

"How am I going to get Pete Rose?"
(Topps trading cards used courtesy of the Topps Company, Inc.)

The job responsibilities were always handed down to the show's young assistants. Mitchell said, "Later on, all the production assistants would go down and get the guests. If they were Mets, they would come right in from next door. The clubhouse was right next to our control room."

One of those production assistants was Steve Oelbaum, who started in 1984.

"It was basic stuff in running to get the guest", said Oelbaum. "That was during the days when the set had that wood paneled look, no pictures, and the desk that I remember well. One of first shows I ever did was when they brought in Lindsey [Nelson], Bob Murphy, and Ralph when all three were elected into the Mets Hall of Fame. It was also the last year of the desk."

Mets Vice President of Media Relations Jay Horwitz has been employed by the team since 1980. In the early years of his tenure, Horwitz was one who had the responsibility of securing the guests for *Kiner's Korner*.

"They [the producer or director] would call the press box when we were winning," Horwitz said, "and they would say, 'You know, if we win, we need Bob [Murphy] in the locker room.' I would go down there, they would probably send somebody over. I would get the guy in the locker room. Before we did any interviews in the locker room, he would do an interview with Ralph. So we would communicate with producer Rick Miner and it director Billy Webb and we would do that."

Horwitz said the respect that Ralph garnered made his job a lot easier. "[The guests] knew they were getting the one hundred dollars, so it was just that Ralph's style was so easy to work with. Ralph earned respect for what he did in his career. You know 369 career home runs. He was a Hall of Famer and there was a respect for what he did," said Horwitz.

After a while, Oelbaum could anticipate who Kiner would want to have on as a guest, even without consulting with him. "After Joe Gallagher left as the producer, Ralph Robbins, who had been a stage manager at Channel 9, came in and was the first producer that I worked under," Oelbaum said. "Ralph [Robbins] would talk to Ralph [Kiner] in his headset and ask what guest Kiner wanted. We always knew Kiner would go hitter first, a Met first, and then a star."

Despite being a long-time Mets' employee, Horwitz also helped booked the guests from the visiting team. "Yeah, they would communicate with me if they were ahead," Horwitz said. "I went to the PR guy with the other team, you know. 'Hey, Ralph needs the interview,' the guy gets a buddy and they would enjoy talking to Ralph. Ralph always had a million notes filled with stories and during the interview he would break out a story and talk to the guys."

"The guys would like to sit down with Ralph because of who he was. The players loved to come on *Kiner's Korner*. Tom Seaver was so overjoyed because Ralph gave him fifty bucks," Webb said. "Seaver would say 'This is something I won't have to show Nancy' [Seaver's wife]."

"Everybody that came on from Pete Rose to Willie Mays to Seaver enjoyed it," said Mitchell. "Seaver was always a great guest to come on. Seaver and Ralph had a mutual relationship, mutual friendship for each other. It was always a positive atmosphere. Ralph was never negative on any of his guests. He was always positive. Whatever the winning team was, we'd go and get the guest from the winning team, which was great. Sometimes today, some of the locals don't do that. They just do their team. If their team wins, they do it, if not, boom, they don't talk."

Tom Seaver, " Always a great guest."
(via Wikimedia Commons)

The venue for the show was anything but lavish. According to Gallagher, the set was not an extravagant one, but it was practical. "Comfortable chairs formed in a 'L' shape with Ralph, as you looked at it, on the right hand side and room for somebody on his left and a couple of people on his right," he said. "There was a Met or baseball logo and a couple of pictures."

The earliest shows were broadcast from the Polo Grounds and that made for a logistical nightmare. "We had hoped to have Casey Stengel on but we wanted to have a winner on. Casey wouldn't be happy coming on if they had lost, which they did," Gallagher said. "The Polo Grounds was basically 'football shaped,' and the clubhouses were way out in center field. The set was in the stands behind home plate. I sent somebody out to get Stan Musial for the post-game show and Stan, when the game ended, he headed right to the clubhouse. He wasn't thinking post game. This was the beginning, we hadn't established a reputation with the players yet. I picked up the phone and I called the clubhouse, got the visiting clubhouse man on, I said, 'Can you get Stan Musial to come in?' and he was already in the shower. 'So Red Schoendienst, can he be on?'

It was great. Red Schoendienst was not a superstar," said Gallagher, "but he was a super guy and a very popular guy. We could see him on camera running in from deep center field to the home plate area to be on the postgame show."

In the early years, a pre-game *Kiner's Korner* was featured. Gallagher said they wanted to come up with a feature that would include kids and was based on a show that the Brooklyn Dodgers used to do.

"For the Saturday pre-game *Kiner's Korner*, we adopted an imitation of the old *Happy Felton Show*, said Gallagher. "Happy Felton had kind of a [baseball] clinic for the Dodgers pre-game show. There were kids on the show and one or two players, and they had a little clinic. It was a very well received show and the Dodgers' games had been on WOR-TV, so that was a tie-in as we were on WOR. We would have kids from the New York area on the pre-game show."

Gallagher said they would incorporate a player as part of the show. "We put Ralph up in the booth and he introduced the show and we would have the player on the field with the kids," said Gallagher, "and the player would be wearing the headset and holding a microphone. So then the player took it from there and he would do a little bit of how he hit and so forth."

Neil Best said the interaction with Kiner was so natural. "What made it work early, so it was different from a lot of shows even then and certainly compared to now, was that Ralph was so famously the coolest guy in the world", Best said. "His panache when he was younger was based upon who he was dating, his baseball prowess, and also just his personality. He was so unimpressed—not unimpressed in a bad way but unimpressed—with these famous athletes he was talking to, which ended up making it much more conversational."

According to Best, the show worked because, in many ways, Kiner was on the same level of stature as his guests. "You didn't get that sort of breathless, kind of, 'Oh my god, here I am, talking to Willie Mays' kind of vibe that you might get from a lot of interviewers," said Best, "particularly ones who weren't Hall of Fame jocks.

He was so just kinda like, 'Yeah, well, I'm sitting here with Willie Mays' or Tom Seaver or whoever. Just kinda having a chat and it wasn't like he was pretending to be unimpressed, he really was unimpressed because he was Ralph Kiner. Why should he be in awe of any of these other people? I think that in his own weird Ralph Kiner way, that helped make the show what it was, which was just him talking to fellow baseball stars."

New York Times sports and business reporter Richard Sandomir said Kiner's natural ability to broadcast baseball made it work. "Ralph knew baseball. He was a terrific player and obviously very astute, both about the ins and outs of baseball and the history of it," Sandomir said. "It really showed. He let the players be the players. Whether they were the Mets or the visiting team, he let them be themselves. He didn't steer them into things. He wasn't trying to trick them into saying things. It was just like, 'How did you make that play?' and 'Why did you do that?'"

Sandomir said the simplicity of the show made it work. "I remember how lo-tech it was, nothing was hi-tech at that time but *Kiner's Korner* was lower-tech than most lo-tech." It was in a cramped studio but it always seemed so comfortable because Ralph could not be ruffled. Ralph just went with the flow. He was not truly a professionally trained announcer. They put no money into production values; it didn't matter. It was Ralph talking baseball with anybody who they roped in to get there. It was always endearing. You always knew you might learn something; you might laugh, you might hear something you never heard before. Ralph in his non-professional way was as astute as anybody who came up the normal broadcasting way. There aren't many people who can get away with that, and he could," said Sandomir.

Webb said directing Kiner on the show was easy but occasionally it became a challenge. "Oh yeah, when I asked, 'Ralph move to your right a bit' and he'd move to his left."

Money was a bit of an issue as well, though the amounts were small by today's standards. Ralph reportedly was paid $50.00 per show. In the 1970's, Kiner held out for $75.00.

The dispute led to Kiner's threat to boycott the broadcast. "Ralph was in negotiations. It was opening day and Ralph told the station, 'Unless you give me what I want, I'm not going on.' What happened was, Ralph never went on and was replaced by Bob Murphy," Webb said. (Bob Murphy and Lindsey Nelson became "fill-in" hosts until Ralph returned.) Eventually, things were worked out and Ralph returned to the broadcast booth.

Gary Myers, who is a well-known NFL football columnist for the *New York Daily News*, was paid $25.00 per game to work on the broadcasts and the post-game show as a production assistant. He worked during the summers of 1974 and 1975. Prior to that, he'd been a vendor at Shea Stadium.

One of Myers' responsibilities was to provide an updated scoreboard for the game telecast and for the scoreboard portion of *Kiner's Korner*. "During the course of the game, I would update the batting averages, home runs, RBI's from the *Kiner's Korner* studio. Those stats were on a screen and the numbers you would turn on a knob to the appropriate number for home runs, RBI's and batting average. It was like on a black screen," said Myers, "and you'd put the guy's name up there. It was on a card and there were hooks or whatever that you'd put it on and then it would be 'super-imposed' on the screen. So after every at-bat, we'd update the batting averages. Me and another guy did it."

It sounded easy but there were some difficulties. "Sometimes when I wasn't fast enough, my hand would like go up on TV. That would really only happen if there was a pinch-hitter then we couldn't do it fast enough," Myers said. "The director, Jack Simon, who was just fantastic, would always warn us at the beginning of the season that 'You gotta be quick because I'm quick. As soon as the guy steps into the batter's box, I wanna be putting his numbers up there.'"

After the game was over, Myers had to get the scores ready for Kiner on *Kiner's Korner*. "During the course of the game I would keep the "running inning-by-inning tallies," Myers said. "All the out-of-town games would come off the ticker. In between innings, I would update every game on the score sheet that I had. The pitching changes, home runs, the inning-by-inning score. I would have a board all set up before the game. It was like on an easel. You know, 'who's playing who' and then I'd put the line score up if the game was over or the partial score if it wasn't. I would hand Ralph my score sheets so when it came time to read the scores after the game, it was the last part of *Kiner's Korner*, he'd be reading off my score sheet. Once again, they would super-impose the scoreboard on the screen."

The show would come on pretty quickly after the game was over, so Myers had to be ready to get whatever guests Ralph wanted. "He was definitely down in the control room when the game was over," Myers said. "When the game was over they'd almost go directly to *Kiner's Korner* and there wasn't much of a recap on the air on TV and just go to Ralph. As soon as he would come down, I'd say 'Okay, if nothing changes, who do you want for the show?' It usually would be two guests and it was fifty dollars. I know it was fifty dollars because I was the one who handed them the money."

In the 1980s, WOR enhanced the look of the show with a new studio. "We built a new set because we'd change it every once in a while," Mitchell said, "and I was involved with the design of the set. A big desk was there.

Ralph sat behind a desk. At the time, we put a chroma key [a technique for layering video images based on color] over his shoulder so we could put shots in that chroma key over his shoulder."

The studio was new but it wasn't roomy. "The one right next to the control room, it [the set] was about as big as a closet," Webb said. "They had a window in the control room where you could look in and watch *Kiner's Korner*. There would be, I'd say, maybe ten or fifteen people during every post game show that would watch *Kiner's Korner*. It was kinda cool."

Mitchell said the show evolved to a point where the set needed to be larger. "Every few years or so, we'd have to change this, we'd have to change that. We brought a desk in so we could fit two or three guests and Ralph. Ralph became the anchor. That was the time in television where things were changing from just sitting there on a chair, a platform to kind of a desk in the background," said Mitchell.

Lindsey Nelson left after the 1978 season so Kiner worked with a number of other on-air partners including Steve Albert, Art Shamsky, and Lorn Brown. The chemistry wasn't there as it was with the original trio. Brown was considered "too bland" for baseball on TV in New York. *New York Post* sports columnist Phil Mushnick said Brown literally put Kiner to sleep. "He [Kiner] would be rocking back on his chair and he almost fell because Brown would put him to sleep," Mushnick said. "He wouldn't stimulate him."

According to Mushnick, former player and Hall of Fame broadcaster Tim McCarver re-energized Kiner and brought the best out of him during the broadcasts. "That was the best thing McCarver ever did,"

Tim McCarver "added twelve years to *Kiner's Korner.*"
(*Bret Linford, via Wikimedia Commons*)

Mushnick said. "He stimulated Kiner. He made Kiner really enjoy doing games with him."

"I'd like to think that was true," McCarver said. "My sole job was not to energize Ralph but it was to draw out of him those stories that he told in the press room that fell on deaf ears perhaps when he was on the air. I enjoyed the stories and I encouraged those stories and that's why Ralph and I got along together."

McCarver's humility and respect for his partner made them mesh on the air. "With Phil [Mushnick] talking about me energizing Ralph, I consider that a real compliment because that means that Ralph considered me a contemporary, while I wasn't," McCarver said. "Therefore, when you're a contemporary when you're not, that shows something about both of you I think and that's why I was so proud to be a part of that."

McCarver sat next to Ralph Kiner for sixteen years but their combined knowledge of the sport exceeded a much longer stretch of baseball history. "My playing era which began in 1959 but Ralph's was over in 1955. We linked these generations of baseball fans together to where it made sense as a partnership," McCarver said. "Where Ralph's career ended, mine began. When you think about it we covered baseball from the war [WW II] through the Korean conflict, through the Vietnam War. All those were over when we started announcing together but then we added another sixteen years so you're talking about close to sixty years of baseball history combined with the two of us. We put it to good use and that was our intention."

McCarver said their camaraderie was special. "What impressed me [about Kiner] was that we got along so well. I had no idea whether Ralph got along with anybody up to that time. Looking back, I can't imagine how he didn't," Kiner's longtime partner said. "It was Lindsey [Nelson]and Ralph, and Bob Murphy in the beginning and Murph and Ralph were still there. Lindsey was teaching I believe at the University of Tennessee at the time. Ralph was so easy to get along with and such a gentleman in every respect. We laughed together and that's what was largely part of our broadcast."

McCarver said he and Ralph had the freedom to dictate the content of the broadcast. "It was loose and anything went," McCarver said, "and we established that very quickly in New York." Our format was that there was no format. We would give the information but there were stories. Ralph had many more stories about the thirties and the forties more than I did because I wasn't born until 1941. The fact of the matter was, and I guess a lot of Mets fans felt that way, the reason we were so accepted was we were loose. It was not a telecast that was built on what a lot of telecasts are built on. It was kind of a 'wild ride' type of deal. The team was ascending and that's really what helped us do the games and I think helped our popularity. We formed part of the team. It was almost a renaissance for Ralph. As [former Mets GM] Frank Cashen said, 'He told a lot of great stories in the press room, but some of those stories didn't get on the air.' Part of my job was to dig deep with Ralph and you didn't have to dig too deep because we got along so well and he trusted me. I trusted him so we had a unique relationship."

"Steve Zabriske [the third member of the broadcast team] was the same way. All three of us had fun. We had fun doing the games. It was fun to see the team rising," McCarver said. The addition of McCarver energized Kiner and helped him get twelve more years out of *Kiner's Korner.*

Howie Rose has worked for the Mets on television and is currently the lead radio announcer on WOR. He is a life-long Mets fan who grew up with *Kiner's Korner.* Rose said the show made an impact on him. "Well, it was just entertainment at first. For a kid who found the Mets from day one at age eight it was a learning experience. It was like going to school. It was 'bare bones' TV so you didn't know what was going to happen. I didn't see the legendary pull down of the set but I've heard of it. [In the early years of the show, Casey Stengel was a guest. When he got up to leave he still had his mic on. As he rose, he pulled the set down.] What really impressed me was the reverence of the people that went on there for Ralph," Rose said. "It really verified to me that this wasn't just some guy calling a game. This was a major figure in baseball."

The career path for the Queens, New York, native took him to a place where he was on-air and worked with Kiner. "Well, it was a different incarnation of the show then," Rose said. "At that point Ralph wasn't capable of handling it by himself anymore, so one of us would co-host. That was different than being a guest but it wasn't quite the same. It

Howie Rose honed his craft under Ralph.
(slgckgc, via Wikimedia Commons)

didn't have a 'feeling of home' early television had because the mid-1960s was early for television."

Rose was able to hone his craft by learning from Kiner. "The dynamic, doing face to face on-camera interviews, is different than broadcasting. What they're doing from halfway up the ballpark rather than being in the bullpen. Simply speaking baseball, if he makes a bad play you say it. Ralph wasn't comfortable addressing [bad plays] on the air because it becomes prosecutorial once the game is over," Rose said. "The guy that was in there just won or unless something out of the ordinary happened, he was always part of a winning performance. You have to reflect on that. It's different than being in the booth. I've learned pretty quickly that doing the game and doing a talk show might just be the difference between driving a car and riding a bike."

In 2010, SNY-TV aired a retrospective look at *Kiner's Korner*. Kiner was one of the co-stars of the show that featured clips and old episodes. Neil Best said the show brought back some good memories for those who grew up with it. "That was when SNY was planning to put some of the old *Kiner's Korners* on their website, so I asked Ralph 'Any thought to reviving the show for television,' Best said, "like putting new shows on television?' His answer was, 'The players are making enough money that they don't need the fifty bucks.'"

Kiner's Korner is credited for being a precursor of today's baseball postgame shows. "It served an important role," said Best. "For a lot of those guys, it was part of the evolution. Before *Kiner's Korner* there certainly were postgame interviews by radio stations or TV stations. That concept was unheard of, but that kind of show with that kind of person, maybe there were equivalents in other markets that we don't know about but certainly in New York, that was a revelation."

"His personality shone through on the tube," said Webb. "He was just a sincere, beautiful man." Kiner would close the show with a signature tag line. As he looked right into the camera, Ralph would say, "If you can't make it back out to the ballpark here, we'd like to see you right back out there."

According to Webb, the after-show activities were most rewarding. "The most fun was not only doing the shows but at night after a game, we'd have dinner. It was McCarver, Zabriske, Kiner, and myself. What a great time," said Webb.

Note:

1. Eddie Lucas; *Jersey Journal*, April 2012.

2

"I should've sent Ralph back upstairs."

AS A BROADCASTER, Ralph Kiner never wanted to be known as a "homer" and that was especially true for *Kiner's Korner*. Kiner wanted to have the "star of the game" as his guest on the show, even if it was from the visiting team instead of the home town Mets.

"What are you doing with that guy on the post game show?"

Sunday, July 26, 1964 @ Shea Stadium

The Mets and Milwaukee Braves were involved in a brawl in the top of the first of the second game of a Sunday doubleheader.

Braves shortstop Denis Menke led off the game with a home run against Mets starting pitcher Frank Lary. The next batter, Lee Maye, was hit by a pitch and started towards the mound. Mets catcher Chris Cannizzaro cut Maye off from getting to Lary but both benches emptied.

Twenty-four-year-old Braves rookie Rico Carty ran out on the field and landed a punch that caught Cannizzaro, but he wasn't done yet. Carty then hit Mets first-baseman Frank Thomas in the jaw.

For some reason, Carty was not ejected. After Hank Aaron flied out to center, Carty smacked a solo home run into the left field stands.

Carty had a terrific day. Milwaukee swept the doubleheader by scoring 26 runs and the rookie was five for ten, with two home runs, three runs scored, and eight runs batted in.

"They were playing the Braves in a doubleheader," said Joe Gallagher, the first producer of *Kiner's Korner*. "In the first game, Rico Carty, who was a good ballplayer, and a physically big and strong man, was also a guy who had professional boxing experience. Carty just peppered Cannizzaro with punches. This was a complete over-match. It kinda developed into a brawl."

No question who Kiner wanted as his guest on *Kiner's Korner* that day. "Carty had at least five hits in the doubleheader, maybe six. I always conferred with Ralph," said Gallagher. "I didn't pick the postgame guests. Usually, it was sort of obvious. We knew who we wanted, but I would always say to Ralph 'Who do you want on the postgame?' To my surprise, Ralph said, 'Get Carty'."

The booking would not sit too well with some members of the home team. "We got Carty, he's on the postgame show, and Ralph is interviewing him and the control room was right next door to the Mets clubhouse," Gallagher said. "Larry Bearnarth, who was the [Mets] pitcher and the player rep, comes into the control room and says to me, 'What are you doing with that guy on the postgame show?' I said, 'cause he had a ton of hits.' Larry just turned around and walked out and didn't talk to me anymore. Bearnarth, I guess he took it personal."

Gallagher said, "We never took the 'homer' attitude toward the broadcasts. We were as far from a 'network approach' as you could get for a home team broadcast. That was something that Lindsey and Murph and Kiner and I had discussions on in spring training in '62. We knew it was going to be a long season but we wouldn't gloss over the errors," Gallagher said.

"Say Hey" says "Hey Ralph"

Friday, May 3, 1963 @ Polo Grounds

It was "Willie Mays night" at the Polo Grounds as the former New York Giant was being honored for his years in Gotham. In the game, the Mets

Willie Mays was on *Kiner's Korner* on Willie Mays night at Shea.
(New York World-Telegram and the Sun staff photographer William C. Greene, via Wikimedia Commons)

dropped a 5–3 decision to San Francisco. On his night, Mays was one for four with an RBI double.

A crowd of over 49,000 showed up to honor the man they called "Say Hey." Mays joined Ralph after the game on *Kiner's Korner*.

Ralph: *"You're only thirty-one years of age. Usually they don't give you a night until you're about forty-one or forty-two. Here you are at thirty-one and you're having a night and you certainly deserved every bit of it."*

Willie Mays: *"The feeling that I had was real great. It's kinda hard for an out of towner to come back and get a night. It's really great."*

Ralph Kiner was one person who could appreciate greatness and he knew he was sitting next to a great one in Mays.

Ralph: *"I don't think this [New York] has ever been a visiting city for you. You broke in here in New York and I know the fans in New York have really more or less considered you as their guy all the way. I don't think San Francisco can hold much claim on you."*

The all-time great became somewhat of a prophet, although it was six years early.

Mays: *"I just hope someday that this team [the Mets] will pick up and have a real good championship club here."*

Talking Hall of Famers

Sunday, June 9, 1963 @ Polo Grounds

Kiner knew when he had something special. This edition of *Kiner's Korner* featured a pair of Hall of Fame players. St. Louis Cardinals' all time great Stan Musial and "the Duke of Flatbush," Duke Snider, who was in the penultimate season of his fabulous career with the Mets. Musial was 0 for 1 with two walks in the first game of a doubleheader that was won by the Mets 8–7. Snider pinch-hit in the second game and struck out as the Cardinals salvaged a split with a 10–4 win.

Kiner set the scene perfectly when he opened the show:

Ralph: *"Well there are not many chances that anyone gets to have two fellas on the show like we have right here now. Stan Musial, of course, you recognize and Stan, we have to apologize. You've been more or less booked for the show a couple of times but this fella (Snider) knocked you out one night."*
Stan Musial: *"I shouldn't say it was good but, of course, as long as 'Duke' does it, it's alright."*
Ralph: *"And our other guest of course, is Duke Snider. Stan, with a total of 471 homeruns in his major league career and Duke has a total of 399. He actually has more than that and I'm gonna talk about that a little later on. There's another fella there with 369. I have to thank Joe Gallagher, our producer, for putting me in the act."*

Kiner's recall and baseball knowledge served him very well in this interview

Ralph: *"Stan is a little bit instrumental in changing the rule in Wrigley Field too. You hit a home run that got stuck in the vines and the fielder couldn't get it out, didn't 'ya."*

Stan Musial appeared with Duke Snider on *Kiner's Korner*, "1,251 home runs in one studio."

Musial: *"That's right, it was several years ago. Of course, it was always a lot of problems around that vines at Wrigley Field but we finally got that squared away. There hadn't been anything there lately, I think."*

Kiner Gets a Loose Cannon to Fire

Thursday, May 30, 1963 @ Polo Grounds

A week after being acquired from the Washington Senators in exchange for first-baseman Gil Hodges, colorful outfielder Jimmy Piersall was a guest on *Kiner's Korner*, following the Mets 2–1 win over the Chicago Cubs.

Kiner's ability to relate to players and to get them to open up served him well during his interview with one of the most vigorous players to ever put on a uniform, Jimmy Piersall, who at one point in his career was hospitalized with "nervous exhaustion," was famous for his on-field antics. Piersall was ejected numerous times throughout his career and was involved in many a brawl with opposing players, teammates, and even fans. The centerfielder battled a bipolar disorder that became the subject of the book and movie *Fear Strikes Out*. Piersall was once quoted

Jimmy Piersall (second from right): "Trouble follows me." Maury Wills is on the left, Milton Berle is to his left, and Willie Mays is to the left of Piersall.
(ABC Television, via Wikimedia Commons)

as saying, "Probably the best thing that ever happened to me was going nuts. Whoever heard of Jimmy Piersall, until that happened?"

Ralph: *"Jimmy, you've been a veteran in major league baseball and a star for the Boston Red Sox, Cleveland Indians, and Washington. Why do you think the people of New York have taken to you so quickly?"*

Jimmy Piersall: *"Well I've had some experiences in the Yankee Stadium that I think they enjoyed and certainly they were on my side with each one. I feel that this is probably what they enjoyed. Things happen when I'm around. [Joe] Cronin, the President of the American League, said I had to leave. Trouble follows me. I don't plan anything but it seems like I don't miss. It just follows me."*

Ralph tried to put Piersall's rep in perspective:

Ralph: *"You're exciting in the field of action. You also take the game very seriously. I'm sure this is one of the reasons why you do have these things happen* *to you. I remember one incident in Chicago where the fans in center field were on you the other way around and you responded by throwing a baseball against the scoreboard after it had gone off. What was that all about?"*

Piersall: *"Well, Ralph, it was one of those days where I was thrown out of the first game after having an 18-game hitting streak and that cost me $250.00 when I threw all that garbage and stuff that was around the ballpark on the field. As you went up the runway, they had all these different pails and I threw them out on the field. When I got back out in the outfield these fans were riding me pretty good but as the game ended, somebody hit me in the ear with an orange. To them it might've been funny but you know how that stings when you get hit in the ear. That's when I fired that ball at the scoreboard. Oh, Veeck [White Sox Owner Bill] got all excited. He called me up said, 'That's my scoreboard' and this and that and he was going to give me a 'going over.'"*

Less than a month after that interview was conducted, Piersall performed one of his most famous on-field stunts when he reached a personal milestone. On June 23, 1963, Piersall hit his 100th career home run off of Philadelphia Phillies pitcher Dallas Green. Piersall decided to honor the occasion by running around the bases backwards. He ran the correct order of the bases but he backpedaled the entire 360 feet

Comedy "Korner"

Monday, April 29, 1963 @ Polo Grounds

Sometimes Kiner would go "outside the box" with the show. After the Mets beat the Los Angeles Dodgers 4–2, two fans who were among the announced crowd of 23,494 would get to experience something special.

Following the game, Buddy Hackett and Phil Foster, two of the top comedians of their day, found themselves sitting next to Ralph Kiner on *Kiner's Korner*.

Ralph opened the show with a "three-shot," which probably caught some fans by surprise.

Ralph: *"Welcome to* Kiner's Korner *and speaking of fans at the ballpark, right now we'd like to speak to Buddy Hackett, who's on my left."*

Hackett (in a soft voice): *"How ya doin, Ralph Kiner."*
Ralph: *"And we'd like to speak to Phil Foster, who's on his left."*

Foster offered the same, soft response as Hackett, and Kiner, like the pro he was, kept the interview moving.

Ralph: *"Phil, how come you're so happy. Here you are smiling."*

You could sense how comfortable Kiner would be with his guests, even when they weren't baseball players.

Foster answered Kiner with a story about something that happened to them during the game.

Phil Foster: *"I tell you why. I got a call from Buddy. He said to me, 'You wanna go see the game tonight. I said 'Yeah.' I had no idea at that time that my friend was gonna come to the park with a Los Angeles [Dodgers] hat."*
Ralph: *"He's got a Met hat on right now."*
Foster: *"So, we got the part and he put on the hat."*

In the background, Hackett said, *"Put both hats on."* (Hackett was wearing two hats on set.)

Buddy Hackett.
(NBC Television, via Wikimedia Commons)

Foster: *"Right before the game, all the new breed started to yell 'Hackett is a fink!' 'Hackett is a fink!' That's when he lost the hat and they chipped in; they bought him a hat."*

After Hackett mentioned that he got a hat in Los Angeles, Kiner got back to the ballgame.

Ralph: *"Now you're talking about Los Angeles, Buddy. We're in New York. We got anything going right here in New York, now how can you talk about LA right here?"*
Foster cut Hackett off: *"I can, they lost."*
Kiner said to Foster: *"You're talking about it the other way around."*

"Stay down, Ralph"

Sunday, May 31, 1964 @ Shea Stadium -Giants 8 Mets 6 (23 innings in second game of longest doubleheader)

In the ninth inning of the second game, the Mets and Giants were tied but Kiner had gone downstairs anyway to host *Kiner's Korner*. The thinking was the Mets were not very good at the time and the game would probably end soon. The game didn't end and Kiner stayed down there throughout the extra innings.

The game lasted 23 innings and the Giants came away with an 8–6 win. "That's one of the mistakes that I made," said Joe Gallagher, the producer of the show from 1962 to 1965. "I kept him downstairs. When you get into extra innings you really expect it's going to end the next inning."

Gallagher said they didn't waver from their usual routine. "Our procedure on the broadcast was Ralph would do play-by-play in the middle innings. He'd do two innings on radio and two innings on TV and he'd kinda float [back and forth] for commentary. At the end of the eighth inning he would come downstairs. He would get ready to do the postgame show. So now we get into extra innings and I keep saying 'Well, the game is gonna end. How can the Mets keep up with the Giants?' But it turned out to be a fabulous game. Galen Cisco pitched almost nine innings of shutout ball until the Giants finally scored."

Gallagher said the one regret that he had during his tenure as the producer was that he didn't let Kiner go back to the booth. "I should've sent Ralph back upstairs. Murph [Bob Murphy] and Lindsey [Nelson] were stuck. They had to do the play-by-play. Lindsey was on TV and Murph was on radio. There was no one to give them a half inning off to go to the bathroom. When I think back on it, I should've done it differently."

No matter how long the game went, there was still a show to do. Gallagher had spoken with Kiner and they decided that even if the Mets lost, they wanted to get a hometown player on as a guest.

"When the Giants finally broke through, they took [Galen] Cisco out and Ralph and I agreed that we should ask Cisco to be on the post-game show," Gallagher said. "I went out to meet him. As he came out through the tunnel, I asked him and he just shook his head, 'no.' He was on the verge of tears. He was a tough guy, he had been a linebacker at Ohio State and a very good one. He was physically kind of a rugged guy and he said 'no' and I apologized for asking him because I could see it was such an emotional time."

Cisco came to me the next day and apologized. I said 'Galen, you don't have to apologize.' I said, 'What you went through was such a great thing.' He had the class to say that he was sorry that he said no," said Gallagher.

The show went on and there were three guests including pitchers Larry Bearnarth and Frank Lary and outfielder Joe Christopher. Despite the long wait, Kiner brought a lot of energy to the show and you could hear it in his comments to open the show that day: "A ballgame that made baseball history right here at Shea Stadium. The longest game ever played in the major leagues, the longest game ever played to a decision in the National League and the major leagues."

After he introduced the guests, Kiner put the game in its proper perspective with some vintage "Kinersims": "The New York Mets set records galore here in the ballgame. The longest double-header in elapsed time in major league history. The longest game in 'lapsed time in major leagues. The longest game in the National League this year in innings. The most innings in a double-header in the major league history of a game. Most strikeouts in a double-header. Longest game to be televised in color, and the longest game to a decision in National League history."

"You think that was for real?"

July 29, 1984 @ Shea Stadium: Banner Day and the "Pregnant Pause"

Bob Heussler is an on-air personality for WFAN Radio in New York and a lifelong Mets fan. Heussler and his wife Marcia (now deceased) were part of a memorable Banner Day promotion at Shea Stadium in July 1984 that prompted a response from Ralph Kiner during the telecast of the event. Mrs. Heussler was in the final stages of her pregnancy when they decided to be part of the festivities between games of a double-header. Despite the fact that it was a very hot, steamy day, the couple wanted to be part of the banner parade.

"I was working at Milford Jai-Alai at the time and we did a lot of work with a local sign maker. I went to the man and said 'I need your help. Here's what we're thinking about. My wife and I want to march in Banner Day. We need you to make a nice long banner in the Mets blue and orange and came up with the idea of 'Future Met Warming Up in the Bullpen'."

"My wife was a heckuva sport and we went down there that day around the seventh inning of game one and it was hot. It was really, really hot. We were tardy so basically it was first show up, first served in line. There had to be about 3500 banners that year. Whatever it was we were near the back of the line and I'm like 'Oh my god, my poor wife', but she didn't blink. So we get in this long line and we're waiting for a very long time."

Heussler said he and his wife suddenly became crowd favorites.

"We had really good seats that day. We had box seats, very close to home plate," Heussler said, "I could hear my friends and I realized what they were shouting about. We were on 'Diamond Vision.' We came in from center field, went down toward home plate on the third base side and we curl up and went up the first base line toward right field. That moment that we were on 'Diamond Vision' was also being shown on Channel 9."

At that point, Ralph and Steve Zabriske (two of the Mets TV broadcasters in 1984) commented on it:

Ralph: *"Warming up in the bullpen."*

Steve Zabriske: *"A young lady with child."*

Ralph: *"You think that was for real?"*

Zabriske chuckled: *"Certainly looked it. Since my wife is expecting in about a month, I have a somewhat experienced eye with which to perceive that I guess."*

Ralph: *"You're considered a professional in that department."*

Heussler said, "He [Kiner] suggested, without saying it, she had a pillow to make it look like she was pregnant."

3

"Jim, do you want to go on with Ralph Kiner?" And he said, 'I'm not going on.'"

IT WAS FATHER'S Day in 1964 and a crowd of more than 32,000 was on hand to witness Phillies pitcher Jim Bunning toss the fifth ever perfect game in the modern era, a 6–0 blanking of the Mets in the first game of a doubleheader.

Joe Gallagher, the producer of the show, was downstairs in the visitors' dugout immediately after the game ended. "We had a routine because no-hitters were not unusual to the Mets," said Gallagher. "Our routine was that we would get the camera in position and Ralph would get in position and I would go get the pitcher. So I went over to the third base dugout where the Phillies were and waited for Bunning to go off the mound, his teammates to slap him on the back and shake his hand. That probably took at least a minute or so."

Gallagher was ready to book his guest. "When he saw us in the dugout I pointed to Kiner and I said 'Jim, do you want to go on with Ralph Kiner?' and he said 'I'm not going on.' I said, 'You're not going on?' He said, 'Well, I want to know what you're gonna pay me.' And I said, 'Jim, we have a gift system, we take care of the players very well.' Then he said, 'Well, that doesn't cover it. That's what they told me in Detroit when I pitched my no-hitter and then I ended up getting nothing.' I said, 'Jim, we're not Detroit.' I said, 'We have a good reputation with the players.' He said, 'Well, I'm not going on.' We were sitting in the dugout talking and I couldn't believe it," said Gallagher. "The fans were calling for him, and his wife and the kids were there too and it was Father's Day. I was about to give up and just walk away and then he said, 'Alright, I'll go on.' He went over and he went on with Kiner and of course he had a big ovation from the crowd when he came back out of the dugout."

Gallagher convinced Bunning to appear on the show because the interview would be broadcast back to Philadelphia. (The game hadn't been televised in Philadelphia.) "To Bunning's credit, he went on and he gave a very good interview. We timed it so that we could give the interview to the Philadelphia stations."

As Kiner conducted the interview, a woman ran out of the stands and ran up to Bunning and threw her arms around him. It turned out to be his wife. For his efforts that day, Bunning received one thousand dollars to go on the *Ed Sullivan Show* that night.

WOR-TV in New York broadcast the game but the tape was deemed lost until a discovery was made in the catacombs of Shea Stadium. Steve Oelbaum, who began working on the show in 1984 as a production assistant and eventually was named producer in 1987, found a tape that contained the last three outs of Bunning's historic day. "In early February, before the baseball season, we would go out and set up the control room for the upcoming season. It was a really cold February day and the guys are moving carts, equipment, and monitors," Oelbaum said. "There was this huge metal door between the control room and the studio and we needed to keep it open to have access. The only way we could do that was to put these two really heavy boxes filled with old two-inch tapes [against the door] to keep it from closing. As we were moving back and forth, my foot goes right into this tape box. Thank god it was winter because it's probably the only reason I still have a foot, so I'm yelling and screaming and in real pain and no one is really paying attention. I looked down at the box just to see what I had hit and I read the labels. The first one says 'Murray the K day at Shea.' There was another tape box behind it with a blank label on it. It was peeled back so I took the label off and there it was, the last three outs of Jim Bunning's perfect game and *Kiner's Korner*.

Oelbaum couldn't believe what he had found. "I am looking at this thing and saying 'What the hell?," said Oelbaum. "This is still here and nobody has touched this tape for twenty-four years and it's being used as a doorstop?"

Like a kid with a new toy, Oelbaum excitedly took the tape to the station. Oelbaum said, "I head to Secaucus [New Jersey] and I bring it to Rick Miner, the director at the time, and he told me to go to the tape room right away and get them transferred because no one used two-inch tape anymore. I get the tape transferred and I am just waiting for the right moment."

Oelbaum waited for just the right moment to surprise Kiner and reintroduce this piece of history to the viewing public. "My plan was to keep this tape in reserve for Father's Day. So on Father's Day, 1988, David Cone two-hits the Phillies. How's that for irony?," Oelbaum said. "Yes, it wasn't a perfect game but it was a two-hit shutout of the Phillies. 'Coney' goes on *Kiner's Korner* and I don't say a word to Ralph other than, 'Ralph, you have to do a quick interview and then quick scores and then say, 'We will be right back.' We come back from the commercial break and director Jeff Mitchell plays the tape with the intro, then the three outs and then Bunning's interview on *Kiner's Korner*."

The release went over big in the studio and on the air. Oelbaum said, "I just remember looking at Ralph's reaction through the whole thing and he was loving every second of it. Just looking at his face, you knew this was the best thing he had seen in a long, long time."

Oelbaum accepted congratulations from his co-workers who, like Kiner, hadn't known about the tape. "Everyone in the crew is stopping by, telling me that was amazing, great job, high-fiving me, slapping me on the back. In the meantime, Ralph packs his bag, goes out the door, lights his cigar and says absolutely nothing. As Ralph walks down the hallway towards the locker room, all the while deep down inside I wanted some sort of acknowledgement from him. About a half an hour later, after all the dust had settled, Ralph is walking down the hall and he yells out to me, 'Olbee.' I look up and Ralph gives me the thumbs up. Right at that moment, I knew that was high praise."

"Doggett came over and said to Sandy, 'Go on with Kiner, I can wait'."

There were some special occasions where Kiner would do a *Kiner's Korner* on the road. On Saturday, June 30, 1962, Hall of Famer Sandy Koufax had just pitched his first career no-hitter against the Mets at Dodger Stadium. Kiner, thanks to his astute baseball knowledge, went downstairs early to prepare to interview the twenty-six-year old southpaw. Since the game was on the road, the home team broadcast would have the first shot at interviewing Koufax.

According to producer Joe Gallagher, "We were televising the game back to New York. Kiner, he just knew [that Koufax would throw a no-hitter]. He had this baseball 'experience' about him. In the eighth inning, I got him down, there's kind of a runway behind home plate at Dodger Stadium. The last out is made and I go over to the Dodgers dugout and wait for Sandy. Sandy is coming towards me and I pointed to Kiner and [Koufax] said, 'I can't go on.' I said, 'What do you mean you can't go on?' 'I have to go on with Jerry Doggett,' who did the post game show on Dodgers radio. I could see his loyalty. Doggett was in the dugout waiting for him. Jerry saw me talking to Sandy, [and] of course he saw Kiner. Doggett came over and said to Sandy, 'Go on with Kiner. I can wait'."

Sandy Koufax.
(N.Y. Public Library Picture Collection, via Wikimedia Commons)

"A little bit of a struggle there . . ."

There was no questioning Kiner's knowledge of the game, and sometimes he would pull no punches.

Tom Seaver made a triumphant return to the team on April 5, 1983. In 1977, Seaver had been dealt to the Cincinnati Reds but rejoined the Mets in '83 and started Opening Day at Shea Stadium against future Hall-of-Famer Steve Carlton and the Philadelphia Phillies.

Seaver pitched six scoreless innings while reliever Doug Sisk pitched the final three and earned the win, but not without a scare. The Mets were leading 2–0 in the top of the ninth when a walk and a single put runners on first and second with one out and slugger Mike Schmidt coming to the plate. Sisk got Schmidt on a fly-out and struck out Tony Perez to preserve the win.

After the game, both Seaver and Sisk joined Ralph on *Kiner's Korner*. Seaver's spot took up most of the show but then Ralph introduced Sisk. "We have with us right now Doug Sisk, who was the winning pitcher in the ballgame and Doug your first [major league win] . . . ." Sisk said, "Yep" and then Ralph hit him with a line that caught him by surprise. "A little bit of a struggle, wasn't it, at the end there?" Ralph asked referring to the ninth-inning tension. Sisk responded, "Yeah, a little bit. I just wanted to get them out in order but it didn't work out that way."

Ralph knew he was being tough with Sisk so he cushioned the blow with his analysis of how the inning developed. "Well you got the first man out then walked a tough man, Joe Morgan," said Ralph. "Mike Schmidt was probably the key to the inning when you got him on one pitch to fly to center."

"He looked at me and I said, 'No curveballs'

In June 1965, New York City Mayor Robert Wagner announced he would not run for a fourth term. Joe Gallagher saw a potential guest when Wagner attended a Mets game at Shea Stadium against the San Francisco Giants. "Wagner made an announcement that he was not going to run for re-election, which was national news because he was a

Robert Wagner: "No curveballs."
(New York World-Telegram and the Sun staff photographer Albertin, Walter, photographer. derivative work: Tilden76, via Wikimedia Commons)

potential vice-presidential candidate. He made the announcement and then refused interviews," Gallagher said.

"The Mets were playing the Giants at Shea. Wagner was a long time Giants fan and he shows up at the game with his girlfriend. They're sitting in one of the boxes alongside the press box, so I said, 'We've got to at least try to get him on the postgame show.' I went up to the press area where he was. The police were guarding the box. Somehow, the door was open and he turned and he saw me and he knew who I was so he told the police to let me in. I said, 'We'd like to have you come in with Ralph Kiner on the postgame show.' He looked at me and I said 'no curveballs.' He asked 'When do you want me to be there?' I said 'I'll come get you in the seventh inning,' and I did. Ralph didn't really ask him but he sorta asked him why he wasn't [running again], and they kinda got into it so we had a scoop."

Pirates make Kiner walk the "prank"

In the 1970s, longtime Pirates broadcaster Bob Prince once co-hosted the show with Ralph. Prince was known as a fun-loving person. He was a smoker and a social drinker. In 1957, Prince jumped into a swimming pool from the third floor of the Chase Hotel in St. Louis on a dare from Pirates third baseman Gene Freese.[1]

Joe Gallagher recalled the co-hosting episode. "The Pirates are playing at Shea. They would take our feed and televise it back to Pittsburgh. Not every game but some games they did. This one game we were televising back to Pittsburgh, we had Bob Prince on with Ralph." Prince says before the game, 'Don't worry about the guests, I've already taken care of that.' I said, 'At least tell me what you've taken care of.' He said, 'I'm gonna have [Jim] Pagliaroni and Don Schwall come on dressed as women.'"

Gallagher went along with the gag. "[The guests] wouldn't be the star of the game that we usually went for. Prince said, 'You can't tell Kiner. It's supposed to be a surprise.' The game ends and Prince gets down to the studio in a hurry and he's there. I left this one door unlocked so the players could come in. They came in and they were all 'dressed' up. They had rings on all their fingers. One of them had a thing on his head that was sorta like a flower pot and they had earrings. They had themselves made up as women."

So they [the players] show up and start talking like women. Ralph is trying to get the show back on baseball. Kiner knew who the players were and went along with the gag. He said, 'Who is the toughest pitcher that you ever saw?' Pagliaroni took his hand made a gesture like he was wiping his eyelashes, he said 'Koufax is a brute.'"

Gallagher was clearly not comfortable with the whole scene and was concerned someone up above would see the show. "Even though I had cleared it with my superior I was worried. As it turned out, [general manager] George Weiss had left early that night so fortunately he didn't see the show. If he had I'm sure there would've been hell to pay.

This is the kind of stuff that Ralph was willing to do."

Kiner's Korner finale at the Polo Grounds

An announced crowd of 1,752 fans showed up on September 18, 1963, to watch the final major league game at the Polo Grounds in upper Manhattan, which had been home to the Mets until Shea Stadium opened in April 1964.

The Mets dropped a 5–1 decision to the Philadelphia Phillies as pinch-hitter Ted Schreiber became the answer to a trivia question. Schreiber grounded into a game ending double-play as the final batter at the Polo Grounds.

Despite Schrieber's dubious achievement, the guest on *Kiner's Korner* that afternoon would be none other than Casey Stengel. Ralph opened the show by touching on Casey's career, both as a manager and a player.

"Well, only one man in baseball at this point who has ever played in the Polo Grounds as a player and still in uniform, in active uniform as a manager and be right here at this television outlet and it's Casey Stengel. Casey going back fifty years. You take in quite a bit of territory when it comes to time in baseball in the Polo Grounds."

Casey answered by taking a "shot" at the media.

"Fifty years ago I can remember this ballpark where they used to have all the newspaper men, they'd be right on the first floor, right back of home plate. So if you got mad at 'em—if they didn't give you a base hit or if they made an error—you'd run over and argue with the newspaper man 'cause he didn't give you a base hit or an error."

Casey continued as only he could by reciting the history of the ballpark in his famous "Stengelese," and Kiner knew not to try and stop him.

"Then there was the right field wall. That's the first concrete that I ever saw in baseball at that time. Every minor league park, there was no stadiums at that time, they were made of wood. Fences were wood. The ballplayers had a terrific time after baseball started because the fact you'd run up to catch a ball against this concrete. You'd turn around and the rebound was a little sudden for 'ya."

New York Post sports columnist Phil Mushnick recalled that one of Kiner's favorite memories from the show came in the first year involving Mets Manager Casey Stengel. "Casey had a special kind of microphone on," said Kiner, "and when he got up to leave, he didn't take it off. He ended up pulling the whole set down. He picked up most of it but no one picked up the cue cards and I had to close the show."

That wasn't the only time that Stengel created an awkward situation for the show.

Happy Birthday, Casey: "I'll never make the mistake of turning seventy again"

Joe Gallagher recalled the time a special celebration was planned for Casey's seventy-second birthday in 1962. "The media, the press, everybody made a fuss over Casey's birthday. His birthday was July 30. In 1960, Casey turned seventy years old. That night, they had a big party at Toots Shor's for Casey. The Yankees threw it. It was a big deal. The Yankees fired Casey [after the loss to the Pirates in the 1960 World Series] saying he was too old," said Gallagher, "and Casey's line was 'I'll never make the mistake of turning seventy again.'"

It's two years later and he turned seventy-two and we're playing a doubleheader in St. Louis [on] Casey's birthday. I call the Cardinals and said, 'We're televising both games back to New York and we're gonna have Casey on [between games] with Ralph Kiner who will be doing the interview and I'm ordering a cake.' I said, 'I would like to see you have the crowd sing 'Happy Birthday' to Casey.' I remember [St. Louis PR director] Jim Toomey said to me, 'Casey is not a Cardinal,' he said, 'we're the Cardinals.'"

"I said, 'Yeah, but he's Casey Stengel, he's an institution, whatever team he's with.' And they bought my argument. They had the crowd sing 'Happy Birthday' to Casey and then Kiner was interviewing him. Now it's getting close to the second game and in those days it was Sportsman's Park and at some point it became Busch Stadium. The visiting team occupied the first base dugout, the Cardinals used the third base dugout. Both teams dressed on the third base side. The visiting team always had to come out through the third base dugout and walk across the field. So now the Mets players are coming out, crossing the field to the first base dugout and Marv Throneberry walks by and Kiner is interviewing Casey. Throneberry says 'Yesterday was my birthday, you didn't have a cake for me.' And Casey's line was, 'We were going to, but we thought you'd drop it.'

Cut It Out: "You made baseball look bad"

Tug McGraw was one of the most colorful characters to ever wear a Mets uniform. The left hander made his debut in 1965 and established himself as a top notch closer. In July of 1973, McGraw coined the famous words "Ya Gotta Believe!" The Mets went on to rally down the stretch of the season to win the NL East and eventually go on to the World Series. McGraw was well known for his wit and outgoing personality so he was a natural for *Kiner's Korner.*

The lefthander had attended a barber college after high school so Joe Gallagher came up with a novel idea. Kiner would get his hair cut by McGraw in the studio while they were talking baseball. The usual chatter that accompanies a visit to the local barber shop was the the inspiration for Gallagher's idea.

"That was a pre-game, it was a Sunday show. It was really based on my growing up in the Bronx in the 1930s," Gallagher said. "A lot of the New York Giants would sublet apartments during the baseball season. Riverdale, New York, was always an upscale neighborhood in the Bronx and there were enough people that went away for the summer, that there were vacancies and nice apartments. Carl Hubbell even owned a home in the Riverdale area."

"They [the players] used to go to the barber shop on Riverdale Avenue and 238th Street," said Gallagher, "to get their haircuts, shave and so forth. The one barber that they went to, a guy named Warren, was also a big baseball fan. When I got my haircut I would talk baseball with Warren. To me when you get your haircut at a barber shop, you're talking about baseball."

Gallagher knew about McGraw's experience with the clippers and thought that would go well with the show, but the idea was nearly squashed by Kiner.

"That was my mentality and when I found out that Tug had gone to barber college and was giving haircuts to some of his teammates, I said to Kiner 'let's have him [Tug] on a pre-game show and he can give you a hair cut,' Gallagher said. Ralph said, 'I'm not gonna let him cut my hair.' I said 'not to worry, I'll bring one of my kids and he can cut his hair' so my son, Bill volunteered and we went out to the park. Ralph showed up Sunday about noontime. He said, 'I changed my mind, I'm gonna let Tug cut my hair,' and I said, 'You son-of-a-gun you spent all your money drinking last night and you need a haircut and you're gonna get one free,' and he said, 'Yeah.'"

Tug McGraw: "Can't turn down a free haircut!"
(*Philadelphia Phillies/MLB, via Wikimedia Commons*)

Little did the producer know that the "higher ups" were watching and did not take kindly to the stunt. "Tug gave him a haircut and they talked baseball," Gallagher recalled. When the show was over, assistant general manager Johnny Murphy was waiting in the clubhouse for Tug and chewed him out. He said, 'You made baseball look bad.' Tug was just a kid so he was a little upset over it. They never said anything to me and as far as I know they never said anything to Ralph."

About the haircut, Kiner said, "It took me about four months for me to grow my hair back."[2]

"He was so honest. I never ever saw him even remotely disrespectful to anyone"

"Absolutely that was the thing that always struck me about Ralph," said Mets broadcaster Howie Rose. "Probably because he was a Hall of Fame player; he had been a national star and he was a Mets broadcaster. I could see why it could be very intimidating. You don't just walk up to Ralph and say 'Hey.' But the truth of the matter is, you could. He was so honest. I never ever saw him be even remotely disrespectful to anyone. I've been with him when a waitress dropped a tray of drinks with him."

Rose said there was one time where he thought Kiner would be disrespectful. "The closest I came was in San Diego when he was puffing on a cigar in the booth. The guy comes in very apologetically," Rose said, "and said 'Sorry, Mr. Kiner, I'm very sorry but there is an ordinance now, you have to put the cigar out.' And Ralph just puts it down and said, 'This used to be a great state.' He didn't look at the guy and say anything condescending. He was disappointed and he said what he said but he never took it out on anyone. That was the Ralph that Gary [Cohen] always talks about, and he'd probably used the line 'He has never been so comfortable in his old skin.' And yeah, every time Gary says it, I say, 'You better believe it.'"

Notes:

1. Wikipedia.
2. Sabr.org/bioproj/TugMcGraw.
3. *Game of My Life Philadelphia Phillies: Memorable Stories of Phillies Baseball* by Bob Gordon (Sports Publishing 2013).

4

"We have as our special guests on the show—obviously, it's 'Gary Cooper.'"

LIKE HALL OF Famer Yogi Berra, Hall of Famer Ralph Kiner is also well known for his malapropisms and misnomers that have come to be known as "Kinerisms."

Kiner rivaled Berra with lines like, "That's what makes baseball, you never know exactly what's going on." When Ralph would read a spot for the sponsor Manufacturer's Hanover Trust, he would call it "Manufacturers Hand-over Trust." Instead of, "It's academic," Ralph said, "It's aca-medic."

"Kinerisms" made Ralph Kiner even more revered to baseball fans everywhere, although it made the originator a little uncomfortable. In his autobiography *Baseball Forever: Reflections on 60 years in the Game,* Kiner addressed the reactions to the 'malaprops.' "When you say thousands and thousands of words, you are going to make mistakes, I don't care who you are."

Kiner owned up to the mistakes and eventually embraced them. "In the beginning, I was sensitive when people called attention to my gaffes because I wanted to be perfect, and not saying what I intended bothered me," he wrote. ""When I realized I couldn't be perfect, I stopped worrying about it and shrugged it off. At least my verbal misplays added humor to the broadcasts, which is usually a good thing."[1]

Neil Best, who authors the column "Sportswatch" for *New York Newsday*, said the mistakes were just "Ralph being Ralph." "That was another thing that went to his 'every-man kind of persona,' even though he was a major star in his day," Best said. "Probably made the players feel they didn't have to come off sounding all perfect and polished if he didn't. The thing of course about that era, they were all on their own. These teams did have public relations' directors in that era but it was not as organized as it is now. Back then, PR guys for a lot of pro teams, their main job was taking the writers out for drinking on the road. The whole idea of micro-managing the players' schedules just wasn't part of it."

Jeff Mitchell, the producer and director of the show in the 1980s said they never tried to correct Kiner. "I remember Manufacturers Hanover was one of the sponsors and at the time, Ralph would call it 'Manufacturers Handover.' It was perfect for a bank: hand over your money."

"It was part of his persona. It humanized him," *New York Daily News* columnist Bob Raissman said. "People who might've laughed, [it]was because he made them laugh, it was funny. He just kept on going on and doing them, not knowing what he was doing and also not making a big deal out of it. There are other guys who had malaprops. Jerry Coleman for instance. He would do similar things but you never heard from these guys who made it their signature. To me, part of his charm was that. Some of 'em are memorable to this day. You talk about the "Yogisms." Well, the "Kiner malaprops" fall into the same kind of realm, almost."

Ralph was so beloved that even the sponsors could shrug off a mistake here or there, although there was one time that wasn't the case. Former catcher Tim McCarver was Kiner's partner for sixteen years on New York Mets telecasts. "There was a woman who called from the advertising agency, and she was complaining about Ralph mispronouncing one of their products that the company represented. It was a switchboard operator from the Mets that answered the phone. The operator asked, 'What broadcaster mispronounces your product?' She said, 'It's a Mister Keener.' She was complaining about him mispronouncing one of their products while she mispronounced his name," McCarver said.

Kiner simply had trouble pronouncing some of the sponsor's products. Said McCarver, "He couldn't pronounce 'Meineke.' (mine-ah-key) 'Meineke Muffler' was another one of our sponsors and Ralph kept referring to it as 'Meen-Key Mufflers,' 'Meineke was 'Meen-Key,' Amoco was 'a'-mo-co' and the funniest one was 'Manufacturers Hanover Trust.' He called it 'handover' and 'hangover.'"

"I had to take him off doing billboard," said Bill Webb, the award-winning director of *Kiner's Korner*. 'Manufacturers Hanover' became 'Manufacturers Handover.'" I told him, 'Ralph, you can't say 'Handover.' That's a bank for 'Christ-sakes'."

New York Post columnist Phil Mushnick recalled how Ralph dealt with a paint sponsor. "When *Kiner's Korner* was brought to you by Martin Paints, halfway through the show he would do the read for the Martin Paints dealer. 'Check your listings for your local Martin Paints dealer.' Whoever he was interviewing prior to that read would become a guy named Martin," said Mushnick. "In other words he had [Phillies manager] Gene Mauch on and right after he read about Martin Paints he goes, 'I'm back now with Gene Martin.'"

McCarver said his "flubs" were not mocked but were a part of what made Kiner well liked by his public. "His malaprops were famous. You'd have to go back through the world of malaprops to get the flavor of what Ralph was saying," McCarver said. "I remember we had 'American Cyanamid,' which was a company that was gonna be our sponsor. As a trial, they had this promotion, 'Call to the Bullpen.' It was the first time we'd ever done anything with 'American Cyanamid.' The ratings were huge in those days. I mean just monster ratings. We were in San Diego and Ralph was doing the play-by-play. I used to look at the sponsor's names before. It was common for guys to do that but Ralph didn't do that. He didn't think it was that important. If he ran into a word that he was gonna mispronounce, whatever he saw, he said. It was a 'Call to the Bullpen' and the stage manager would give us the cue. This 'Call to the Bullpen' is brought to you by 'blank' or this 'Call to the Bullpen' is brought to you by someone else or, 'We'll be back after this word from Amoco.' With Ralph he always called it 'a'-mo-co' which is wrong. That day he said, 'This Call to the Bullpen is brought to you by American Cyanide.' So we were advocating that the Mets were either playing so poorly or that we were advocating cyanide pills for our audience. Ralph and I laughed about that. It was painful. I got pains in my stomach from laughing so hard. We came back on the air and we were still laughing.

People realized that those are mistakes that Ralph's gonna make. And in the long run, so what, who cares?"

Mets radio announcer Howie Rose worked with Ralph Kiner on some of the television broadcasts. "At the end of the 2011 season we were doing an on-camera wrap up after the last game and they're rolling in highlights. They get to the September 11th game where Liza Minnelli sang her famous song, 'New York, New York' during the seventh-inning stretch.When I'm on camera I always have my mic in my left hand and my right hand in my right pocket, and Ralph says, 'That was Liza Mizilli.' I was told from day one that you can't laugh. He isn't comfortable with the malaprops and it makes him uncomfortable in the moment,[so] just don't go there. So now Ralph says 'Liza Mizilli,' it's the last game of the year, kinda loose, the producer [is] in my ear piece. He sees me starting to go a little bit," Rose said. He says 'Under no circumstances are you allowed to laugh. You are absolutely forbidden to laugh.' What he was trying to do was to get me to laugh. I probably still have a black and blue mark for how hard I was pinching myself not to laugh. Kevin Meininger was the producer. He tried everything to make me laugh."

"I was doing a game with him one time. We're in Montreal and Lee Mazzilli comes on deck," Webb said. "I said to him on the IFB [a device that allows the director to communicate with the on the air talent] 'That's Mazzilli on deck.' Ralph would respond with 'There's that Maa-zer-ow-ski on deck.' The whole at-bat, he was 'Maa-zer-ow-ski.'"

"He called me probably twelve different names," said McCarver, "I went by a lot of aliases in those days. I was 'MacArthur' and 'McCarthy' and 'McGarver.' I was 'Ted' and 'Tim.' I think he called me 'Jed' once. I don't know where that came from. I don't know where any of it came from and I didn't care. It didn't matter to me; it didn't offend me in any way. I was the guy that Ralph mispronounced my name more than anybody. More than everybody put together."

McCarver said he was honored that Kiner would use him for a "Kinerism." "I considered it as that [an honor] and some guys wouldn't do that, I don't think. I don't they they'd consider it an honor but it was. Ralph thinks so much of me that he forgets my name. It was a wonderful thing; I never considered it anything other than that."

One of Kiner's most famous malaprops was created as a result of one of the most significant trades in team history. In the winter of 1984, the Mets made an historic trade with the Montreal Expos to acquire All Star catcher Gary Carter.

On April 9, 1985, Carter's Mets' debut could not have been scripted any better. The future Hall of Famer slammed a game winning home run off of former Met and Cardinal reliever Neil Allen in the bottom of the tenth for a 6–5 victory that sent the 46,781 fans at Shea Stadium into a frenzy.

Ralph Kiner had his guest for *Kiner's Korner* but Carter would not be alone as he was joined by Mets center-fielder Mookie Wilson who had two hits and a run scored in the game.

After calling Carter's home run on television, Kiner nearly missed the start of that memorable show. "The way they used to do the game was Ralph would come down in the seventh inning," said Steve Oelbaum, the associate producer of *Kiner's Korner* in 1985. "And if the game went to extra innings, Ralph would go back up and do the play-by-play in extra innings."

Oelbaum said, "Right away you know who the guest is going to be. My job as the associate producer is to get Carter, so I go running in there and get Gary, bring him to the studio and we are like two minutes to air." Oelbaum thought he had done his job but the perils of putting on a live television reared its ugly head. "I realize we have one small problem," Oelbaum said. "Where is Ralph? Ralph was still upstairs and there was an elevator at Shea that was far from reliable but they always held it at the end of the game for Ralph so that he could come right down."

A feeling of relief came over the associate producer (who was working his first ever show) when the host finally arrived. "We are all sitting there waiting for Ralph." This is the first show that my name is going to be on the credits and I have no host," Oelbaum said. "Then we see Ralph walking down, carrying that old shoulder bag that he had for longer than I had been alive. I am saying, 'Thirty seconds, Ralph.' He gets to his seat with like ten seconds to air and when the camera went on, it was like he had been there for an hour."

"Well, welcome to Kiner's Korner. *This is the twenty-fourth year of our broadcast and we hope to be bringing you the excitement of the future of*

"Gary Cooper never appeared on the *Korner*, but Gary Carter did."
(*Samuel Goldwyn Company, via Wikimedia Commons*)

the New York Mets. We want to invite you to stay tuned to watch the show throughout the year but I think that's sorta 'extra-su-per-filliss' [instead of 'superfluous'] because as long we have more games like this, it's gonna be you on that end and the stars of the Mets on this end."

Ralph introduced the guests with one of his classic "Kinerisms." *"We have as our special guests on the show. Obviously it's 'Gary Cooper', who, Gary Cooper, that's pretty good,"* as Carter and Mookie Wilson both laughed.

"He said Gary Cooper the whole f***in' show," said Webb. "I would hit him on the IFB and I'd say, 'Gary Carter.' He'd say 'Yes, Gary Cooper.'" "You don't know if Ralph was doing that on purpose or not because he covered himself so well," said Mitchell.

Later, Kiner explained why he said Gary Cooper instead of Gary Carter.

"Glenn Close sang the National Anthem that day, and I was thinking about the baseball movie, *The Natural*, in which Close played Robert Redford's love interest, and *The Pride of the Yankees*, which starred Gary Cooper. Gary was a great sport about it. He came on *Kiner's Korner* after and introduced himself to me as Gary Cooper and even signed a picture to me, "Gary Cooper Carter."

"I don't know at what point the 'malaprops' became endearing," said Richard Sandomir, the TV, Sports, and Business reporter for the *New York Times*. "At the time, there was nobody to criticize him for doing them. He had a 'free ride' until Stan Isaacs started doing his column for *Newsday*," Sandomir said, "and I don't know if Stan criticized him because Ralph didn't intend to do those anymore than Yogi [Berra] intend[ed] to create 'Yogisms.' It was comfortable."

Bill Webb said, after awhile, he gave up on correcting Kiner. "I just let 'em go," Webb said, "You tried to help him but it just became to a point where he either wasn't listening, he wouldn't remember who you're saying or he would be so intent on the conversation he was having with somebody on the air, he just wouldn't correct himself."

Kiner's malaprops are still being quoted to this day. Here are some of the famous ones from over the years:

- "Hello everybody, welcome to *Kiner's Korner*. I'm Ralph Korner."
- "If Casey Stengel were alive today, he'd be spinning in his grave."
- "Solo homers usually come with no one on base."
- "All of his saves have come in relief appearances."
- "On Father's Day, we again wish you all Happy Birthday."
- "That's what makes baseball. You never know exactly what's going on."
- "It's aca-medic"
- "The reason the Mets have played so well at Shea this year is they have the best home record in baseball."
- "The Hall of Fame ceremonies are on the thirty-first and thirty-second of July."
- "The Mets have gotten their leadoff batter on only once this inning."
- "There's a lot of heredity in that family."
- "All of the Mets road wins against the Dodgers this year have come at Dodger Stadium."
- "I think one of the most difficult things for anyone who has played baseball is to accept the fact that maybe the players today are playing just as well as ever."
- "Runner on second, first, and third" (describing a bases-loaded situation)

- "I wonder if he's wearing that number to celebrate his area becoming the 52nd state." (referring to Houston Astros pitcher Julio Solano who wore #52)
- "Oriole pitcher is Martini. Well, not Martini but it's something close to that." (when he read the scores on *Kiner's Korner* and referred to Baltimore pitcher Denny Martinez)
- "Our condolences to the losing team." (when he referenced a local hockey score)
- "Baseball began right here in this very stadium back in 1869." (On Cincinnati's Riverfront Stadium that opened in 1970)
- "Today is the anniversary of D-Day when we won the battle against countries were fighting against." (from a game played on June 6th)
- "This game is being brought to you through the authority of the New York Mets baseball" (when he read a disclaimer).

Kiner's "name game" (former players)

- Former Mets outfielder George Foster was "Keith Foster"
- Pitcher Mario Soto was "Mario Soda"
- Mets third base coach Tim Teufel was "Tim Tooful"
- Outfielder Andy Van Slyke was "Andy Slyke"
- Former Mets pitcher Bruce Berenyi was "Steve Berenyi"
- Outfielder Kevin Bass was "Kelvin Bass"
- Pitcher Len Barker was "Les Barker"

Statistical Kinerisms

- "Nolan Ryan's fastball has been clocked at over 200 miles per hour."
- "Tony Gwynn was named player of the year for April."
- "Mets have a 91.5 success percent rate on steals."
- "It's the second time the Cards have had the leadoff man on with no one out."
- "Mets and Expos have met six times with the Mets winning three and the Expos two."
- "Don Sutton lost thirteen games in a row without winning a ballgame."

- "Mookie Wilson was caught stealing on an error."
- (Bill) "Doran's average is way under the nerm."
- "Kevin McReynolds stops at third and he scores."

In-game Kinerisms

- "Two plays by Danny Heep and the Phillies are out in order and the score at the end of ten, it is the New York Mets three and the New York Mets tied up with the Phillies who have three."
- "Two-thirds of the Earth is covered by water. The other third is covered by Garry Maddox."
- "It's like watching Mario Andretti park a car." (On Phil Niekro's knuckleball)
- (Pat) "Zachry is the kind of batter who can strike batters out with a change up."
- "There's a ground ball hit on the ground to shortstop."
- "The Pirates won eight of their one hundred and two losses against the Mets last season."

Note:

1. *Baseball Forever: Reflections on 60 years in the Game* (No) by Ralph Kiner and Danny Peary(Triumph Books, 2004).

5

"What's your wife's name?"
'Mrs. Coleman, and she likes me, Bub.'"

WHAT'S A POSTGAME show without guests? Good or bad, colorful or bland, throughout the years the guests made for some memorable moments when they sat down on *Kiner's Korner*.

Clarence "Choo Choo" Coleman

Choo Choo Coleman, "urban legend"
(Topps trading cards used courtesy of the Topps Company, Inc.)

Saturday, August 4, 1962 @ Polo Grounds
Mets 9 Reds 1

Clarence "Choo Choo" Coleman was known mostly for his colorful nickname. The left-handed hitting catcher had a modest four-year big league career but played three of those with the Mets.

Coleman's had a famous sit down with Ralph Kiner on *Kiner's Korner*. "I was afraid to have him on," Kiner said, "because he wasn't at all conversational and when he did talk he called everybody 'Bub.'" To set Kiner's mind at ease, the producer booked a second guest.

To get the interview started, Kiner asked Coleman, "Choo-Choo, how did you get your nickname?" His response was, "I don't know 'Bub,' I'm thinking." Kiner than asked, "What's your wife's name and what's she like?" Coleman responded with, "Mrs. Coleman, and she likes me, Bub.'

According to Coleman, that story is a myth. "No, that never happened."

Did you ever get to speak with Ralph about that story which became legendary later on?

"No I never did. You know, I left New York a long time ago, and it's been over fifty years."

Coleman had no prior knowledge of Kiner's career before he went on the show.

"No I didn't, I didn't know him at the time you know. I didn't know I was talking to a Hall of Famer."

The former Mets catcher remembered that he was taken to a make shift studio.

"It was upstairs at the Polo Grounds."

Every guest got some sort of parting gift for being on the show. Do you remember what you got?

"No, I didn't get anything. Getting to be on the show, I won the game for the Mets when we played Cincinnati at the Polo Grounds. That was my gift."

Ron Hunt

Friday, April 19, 1963
Mets 5 Braves 4 @ Polo Grounds

Ron Hunt played for the New York Mets from 1963 to 1966. The second-baseman has the distinction of being the first Met to start an All-Star Game when he was named to the 1964 National League All-Star team. Ironically, the game was played at Shea Stadium.

In 1963, Hunt was named the runner up to Pete Rose for the National League's Rookie of the Year Award.

Hunt was best known for being hit by pitches. When he retired after the 1974 season, the twelve-year veteran was hit a record 243 times.

Hunt's walk-off, two run double off Braves pitcher Claude Raymond in the bottom of the ninth, led the Mets to a come from behind 5–4 win and a spot on *Kiner's Korner.*

"I remember the studio at Shea Stadium being right down the hall from the clubhouse. I am pretty sure you would exit the clubhouse and turn right and it was down a couple of doors. It was just a little studio with a

Ron Hunt: "He talked the game well because he played the game well."
(Topps trading cards used courtesy of the Topps Company, Inc.)

couple of chairs, a few cameras. I don't remember who came to get us. I remember he asked us good questions, none of that bulls**t that they ask today. It was about baseball and not about any other garbage. It was only about what was on the field. I remember Don Drysdale saying, 'Whatever you do off the field is your concern but once the uniform is on it was to be 100 percent baseball. Play the game right,' and that's the way I did it and Ralph respected that."

Hunt didn't play the first six games of the season but after his third career game, he was already on the show.

"I was honored to just be in the majors. Larry Burright was the second baseman. Ralph asked me when I took over, and I told him the same thing I told Casey, when I ran across him in the clubhouse at Forbes Field. I said to Casey, 'Ron Hunt # 33 second base', because he didn't remember names just numbers. He said, 'Yes son, what can I do for you?' I said Well, Larry Burright isnt doing a very good job offensively or defensively at second, maybe this would be a good chance for you to see if I could play or not.' And he said, 'Son, you want to play that bad, then you play tomorrow.' So my first game was the next day in Cincinnati and when we got home and I got on the show, Ralph brought that up and we talked about that, just real businesslike, not so much about playing just my thoughts on getting a chance to play. Kiner was a ground-zero type person. He talked the game well because he played the game well. He played the game right. He played the game clean. He wasn't looking for dirt on the players. He was just looking for common sense and he asked common sense questions that even a rookie could answer. My education isn't that great so if he started using them big words he would lose me."

Hunt was flattered to be chosen to be Kiner's guest after the game.

"Wow Kiners Korner, sponsored by the Nash Rambler. I remember we got a 'little bitty' version of the Nash Rambler and about a $20.00 gift certificate."

"When I was a rookie, it was really an honor [if anyone talked] to me. The big honor was just getting to sit with these great veterans who I had watched at home on TV for years and then getting Duke Snider to take me under his wing like I was his brother. That made the whole start of my career. The announcers were real good to us. Kiner never tried to stab you in the back like these guys today."

Tim Harkness

Sunday September, 1963 @ Polo Grounds
Mets 6 Braves 4 (16 innings)

Tim Harkness' major league tenure spanned four seasons, two with the Los Angeles Dodgers and two with the New York Mets. The highlight of Harkness' career occurred in this early September game during the Mets second year of existence. The first-baseman slammed two home runs including a game winning, two-run blast in the bottom of the 16th inning and it landed him a spot on *Kiner's Korner*.

"We all knew about the show. We knew that he would take the so-called stars of the game and have him on the show. We all knew that we had a shot at being on once in a while. If you did something real good in the game, a big hit or a good pitching performance or something like that you had a shot at it."

After you touched home plate with the "walk-off" homerun, how did you know that you would be on the show?

"As soon as the game was over, you were informed that they would like you to go on the show. They would take you to this little studio, out in the old clubhouse at the Polo Grounds that was way out in center-field where Willie

Tim Harkness "was a big fan of 'King Korn stamps."
(*Topps trading cards used courtesy of the Topps Company, Inc.*)

Mays made that famous catch [in the 1954 World Series]. It was about five minutes after the ball game at most. I was pleased to be picked, as everyone wanted a piece of that."

Harkness was thrilled to be chosen to sit down with Ralph in the *Kiner's Korner* studio.

"I don't remember it being overly bright in there. I remember sitting there watching the replay of the two home runs I had hit. It was a big thing because back then you didn't get to see replays. It's not like today where the guys can sit and watch themselves all the time, which is a great advantage for today's ballplayers as you can see what you are doing wrong. I remember sitting there, looking at myself, and thinking, 'Wow, that's a long swing, much longer then I thought.'

Kiner had played his last game nearly eight years prior to this interview. Harkness admitted he was somewhat unaware of the impact Kiner made on the sport.

"Unfortunately, no. Not to the extent we should have. We all knew about him. I had read about him when I was a kid. I know they had a terrible ball club for many years that he played in Pittsburgh, but he was a star. He was the guy who stood out over everyone there. I think even to this day he is so underrated as a hitter. You add the fact that he played in Forbes Field where it was 365 feet down the line. He really earned every home run he hit. We all knew he was a great hitter, but none of us gave it a second thought. It really is such a shame, when I look back at the fact that we never took advantage of getting baseballs signed by all the greats we saw at old timers games, or guys like Ralph."

Harkness said the gift for his appearance was put to good use.

"I don't really remember the parting gift from the show. It may have been fifty bucks or a gift certificate, which was a big thing because I think the top salary on our team at the time was $60,000. What I do remember most about those days was one of the sponsors was 'King Korn Stamps.' If you did something good like hit a home run, you got like 1,000 stamps, and if you hit a grand slam, you got 10,000 stamps. If you pitched a shutout you got 1,000, and I recall at the end of the season all the guys going and cashing in and getting washers and dryers and stuff like that."

For Harkness, sitting down with Ralph Kiner on *Kiner's Korner* gave him a different perspective about the man.

"I just thought he was hilarious, he was just a very, very funny guy. He had a tremendous sense of humor and I always looked forward to that. He was so laid back that you just really looked forward to talking to him, plus you were on after a game that you did something pretty good so you were already feeling pretty good about yourself. It was always positive and he would ask about the pitch you got the hit off of and that was the best part. Just talking hitting with him because he was such a wonderful hitter in his day."

Ron Swoboda

April 14, 1965 @ Shea Stadium
Astros 7 Mets 6 (11 innings)

Ron Swoboda played six of his nine major league seasons with the Mets.

Swoboda is best known for making one of the greatest catches in World Series history. In Game Four of the 1969 Series against the Baltimore Orioles, Swoboda saved the game with a diving, back hand catch of a drive off the bat of Orioles third-baseman Brooks Robinson. The tying run scored but the Mets went on to win the game and the Series. Many observers felt that catch was the turning point of the Series that helped the "Miracle Mets" score one of the greatest upsets in World Series history.

Ron Swoboda (left) with former Met Daniel Murphy (Mark Rosenman)

Swoboda's first major league home run came as a pinch-hitter and despite the Mets' losing in extra innings, he joined Ralph Kiner on *Kiner's Korner*.

"I'm sure I went on as a rookie a couple of times. I know my first home run, maybe I had a couple of decent games."

Kiner's Korner was mostly broadcast after home games. Swoboda said he missed out because of his success away from Shea during the 1969 championship season.

"You know, I'm not sure I went on too much in 1970 but it seemed like, in 1969, everything good I did was on the road."

Like many fans, Swoboda is sorry that past episodes of *Kiner's Korner* are nowhere to be found.

"I don't recall anywhere we can see it. I wish I did. I couldn't remember one question."

Swoboda had a memorable game in September of 1969 when he hit two home runs and drove in all four runs in a 4–3 win in St. Louis. Cardinals pitcher Steve Carlton gave up both homers and took the loss despite a major league record 19 strikeouts. Swoboda said Kiner was the driving force behind his great day.

"Ralph worked with me one time. I wish I asked him more. The hitting cage in St. Louis had that little machine with two wheels and you can throw a little slider on it. I asked him to come down and look at my swing. I was kinda in the weeds. Feeling like I wasn't doing it, just didn't know where to go next. He would say, 'Move your hands back,' 'How does that feel?' 'OK, good.' That was right before I hit two home runs."

Swoboda was eternally grateful to receive the hitting tips from Ralph Kiner.

"Knowing that the best day I ever had was after I asked him to look at my swing a little bit. People in the game will tell you the best thing you can do for a hitter is to just tell them it's a good swing. Just boost them, give them extra hitting with someone looking at you. I know that you have more confidence and I'm getting the bat around a bit better. When we walk out of the cage and he says, 'That's a swing we can use. Be aggressive and don't swing too much.'"

Swoboda said one of the most lovable things about Ralph was his stories.

"He was wonderful to listen to. I've done enough story-telling in my life. Stories get tighter and when you get on a roll you can tell them pretty well and Ralph could. His stories were the absolute best."

Do you remember one story that stood out?

"My favorite story involved the actress, Jamie Lee Curtis. He [Kiner] went out with Janet Leigh, her mom, back when he was one of the most eligible players. He could have modeled. He was a California guy. One day, Jamie Lee Curtis was coming through the broadcast area and Ralph came out and popped his head out there. I don't think she was looking for him but he said, 'Jamie Lee, I dated your mom' and she looked at him and said, 'Daddy'. Never missed a beat. We should all live our lives like that. It was so funny when I told that. He didn't forget anything."

Swoboda said he still follows the team and enjoys the broadcasts with Howie Rose.

"Oh yeah, I love Howie, man. I text him every once in a while. When they are going good and sometimes going bad, Howie's feel for it is good. I'm a Met fan and I care."

Ed Charles

Tuesday, July 4, 1967 @ Shea Stadium
Mets 8 Giants 7

His nickname was "The Glider," and he was best known for being a member of the 1969 World Champion "Miracle Mets." "E-Z" Ed Charles played a modest eight years in the major leagues, his final three with the Mets.

Charles, who was acquired earlier in the 1967 season in a trade with Kansas City, earned his spot on *Kiner's Korner* after his three-hit game led the Mets to an 8–7 victory on Independence Day as they beat Hall of Fame Giants pitcher Juan Marichal.

Charles was not familiar with the show before he was a guest:

"Not at all because I had come over from Kansas City in 1967 and then played the last three years of my career with the Mets. I retired in 1969 after we won the World Series, and over the three year span, I did have occasion

Ed Charles: "Never throw a slider to the glider."
(Mark Rosenman)

to do the show, but I did not have knowledge of the show until I arrived in New York."

How did he know that he was selected?

"One of Ralph's staffers would come and get us and escort us over to the studio. If I remember correctly, the time that I was on, the studio was next to the visiting clubhouse, so it was just a matter of walking through the Mets clubhouse over to the studio."

What did he think when he first got on the set?

"I thought I had made it to Hollywood! I didn't have any big reaction, because, during my five years in Kansas City, I had been before the cameras many times before. In some respects it was just another day at the ballpark, but being there just meant I did something good that day and there was a feeling of happiness that you were chosen to be on the show."

Charles said his teammates did not view him any differently after he appeared with Ralph:

"We all just felt like it was a privilege to be on. To have done something to warrant being on the show meant you were productive that day. Naturally we went about doing our business of trying to win a ballgame and you do the best you can. You don't look to get on the show, but when you get the call you go on the show."

"The Glider" knew that he was sitting next to baseball royalty.

"Ralph was in the National League and I was primarily an American League player. I knew of him by reading about him in the paper. I never got to play against him, but when I got to the Mets and really got to know him, you just couldn't help but like and respect the guy. He was very personable and I was lucky to consider him one of my friends."

Of course, there was the parting gift.

"A gift certificate to a nice Manhattan restaurant, which was great. You could take your wife. It was just a really nice thing, an extra bonus for having a good day at the park."

Charles appearance on the show produced a favorite moment where his nickname began to stick.

"I would say there was any one moment, but Jerry Koosman had given me the nickname 'The Glider.' When I was on Kiner's Korner the question was raised as to what pitch did I hit for a home run off of Juan Marichal, and I just would always answer 'a slider' no matter what the pitch was. The next thing I know Bob Murphy, the play by play man, picked it up and he started saying 'Never throw a slider to the glider' and it just took off. Fans when they see me they just holler, 'Hey glider, how are you?' It just took off. Even today fans still call me 'Glider.' I get fan mail, people want me to autograph pictures, cards or baseballs and they ask me to put 'Glider' on it. So I think that would have to be my favorite moment because of that."

Saturday, July 14, 2007, was Ralph Kiner Night at Shea Stadium. During the pre-game ceremonies, Mets announcer Gary Thorne read a poem entitled "A Tribute to Ralph Kiner" that was written by Ed Charles, the Mets' unofficial poet laureate. Ed allowed us to include it in the book.

One Moment in Time
A Tribute to Ralph Kiner

Life to us is just a moment in time
When we sing our songs and write our rhymes
When we audition for a role upon life's great stage
Then act out the scripts as written on the page

But some might resent the way the scripts were written
No one prefers the role of a loser snake bitten

We would like a role that brings honor and fame
Not some little bit part that belittles our name

For life to us is just a moment in time
Welcome to the big stage without a nickel or dime
We dream lofty dreams like others before
Then set out to achieve them like the ones we adore

But oft-times some of us misread our scripts
And meet with failure for our bumbling little slips
We replace the original scripts for those of our own
Putting our trust and fate in a destiny unknown

For life to us is just a moment in time
A personal struggle to keep our heads above the slime
A daunting task that beclouds our days
Until the curtains are drawn upon our plays

For the songs that we sing and the rhymes that we write
Are but spiritual reflections of our souls in flight
Some soar gracefully and some are like wingless birds
Grounded and stage frightened for frail are their nerves

But you Ralph Kiner are as composed as one can be
Nothing could sway you from the goals that you set for thee
For you aced your audition with a bat and a glove
Then astounded us with spiels about the game that we love

You kept us in touch with the Glory Days of yore
When character not steroids were the hallmark of a pro
When egos were kept in check by codes of conduct
And ostracism befell those who dared act up

So today we pause to celebrate your climb
From the boondocks to Shea to this moment in time
And to say with affection how grateful we are
That you chose baseball and big Shea to fashion your star

For you are an original, a beloved New York Met
A Pirate and a Hall of Famer, as good as they get
For your moment in time is a mighty fine show
And today the Mets family wanted to tell you so

For now you are a legend like Mays and DiMaggio
And all honors upon you today we admiringly and proudly bestow

Art Shamsky

Friday, August 30, 1968 @ Shea Stadium
Mets 8 Cardinals 2

Art Shamsky was a lanky, left-handed hitting first baseman/outfielder who became an integral part of the Mets 1969 Championship team.

Shamsky had seven hits in the three-game sweep of the Atlanta Braves in the 1968 National League Championship Series. He was popular with New York's large Jewish population. During his first season with the Mets, he hit a grand slam off Cardinals pitcher Nelson Briles to key Tom Seaver's thirteenth win and book himself a spot on *Kiner's Korner*.

Art Shamsky: "I would always look at him and knew he was somebody special."
(Topps trading cards used courtesy of the Topps Company, Inc.)

Prior to being on the show, Shamsky was a big fan of Kiner.

"I don't really remember as a visiting player coming into Shea and being on the show. When I first knew of Ralph Kiner, as a kid growing up, I idolized the guy. He was one of the tremendous home run hitters. He was playing for the Pirates, a bad team but in my mind he was one of the great home run hitters. So I had this idolization of him even when I was playing for the Mets, and then I got to work with him as a broadcaster in '79, '80, and '81. So for me it was always such a thrill just having any kind of conversation with Ralph. I don't remember quite honestly as a visiting player any particular game that I would have been on Kiner's Korner, but that doesn't mean I wasn't. I just don't have any specific recollection of being on when I came into Shea as a visiting player."

"Now that I was on the Mets, I knew I could've been on the show. Most of the teams had postgame shows. Some of them were done in the dugout. They would just put a headset on and you would talk to the broadcasters up in the booth or something. My first experience with Ralph on that show was just going into the studio. I don't know if you were ever in the Mets locker room at Shea Stadium and then you had that little tunnel walkway to get to the dugout and there was a little walkway that went around the stadium and took you down to the bullpen. If you went right out of the locker room you would go past a couple of doors, and Ralph's show was in one of those rooms where I believe all the broadcasts were run out of, where the director and all of that other stuff would be. It was all right there with all that kind of stuff going on. It might have been the room next to it but they were very close in proximity. He was the first that I can remember where you actually went to a specific room and went to a set where he would interview you and that was my first one. I remember doing a lot of different shows but that was the first where you really went into a specific studio area to do the show."

For any player, walking into the studio to sit down with Ralph Kiner usually meant they did something positive.

"Yeah, you were feeling good because for the most part you were probably coming off of a good game. I remember a couple of instances, one specific in Cincinnati where I hit three home runs in a row, and was asked to go on a show. We lost the game and I didn't go on. I hit a fourth one in a row and was asked to be on a postgame show and I didn't go on because

I just didn't feel like, you know we lost both games and I didn't feel like it was right for me to be on. That's the way I was but obviously coming off a good game and now you're going to get interviewed by this great player. As a player I wasn't real friendly with Ralph. We would say hello but I wasn't having these long conversations with him, so for me it was an opportunity to sit down one to one. It was a thrill for me because Ralph was such a standout hitter, and a big, big star. When I got to work with him as a broadcaster in those years, I found him to be such an intriguing person and my admiration just grew for him. We became much closer but I found him to be an incredible storyteller. I was in awe of those years when he was in Los Angeles dating all those movie stars, and that's all I needed to hear. For me, I can honestly say that just having a conversation with Ralph, having him ask you questions, and sometimes the questions were redundant but Ralph was Ralph and just to be on his show was a thrill. I remember the set itself wasn't haphazard, but it was kind of a temporary set and sometimes it fell down. It wasn't the best, but it was still Kiner's Korner. *I remember some of the gifts you would get once in a while, coupons and stuff like that, but I didn't do it for the gifts. I did it because I enjoyed having that one to one conversation with Ralph. He was such a big star for me and it was always a thrill to be on his show."*

Were your teammates on the Mets aware of what kind of player Ralph Kiner was?

"Well, I can only speak for myself. I know I was in awe because of his career and I find it incredible that it took him nine years to get into the Hall of Fame with voting, but that's a whole different conversation. I knew about his accomplishments. I knew about him being on all of those bad teams, leading the National League in home runs. I do believe at some point that he had more home runs in a ten-year period than anybody in the history of the game. Mike Schmidt might have broken a ten-year record of home runs that Ralph had for a while. I knew of his accomplishments and when he would come into the locker room I didn't know what everyone else was thinking but I knew that everyone else respected him. Technically we really didn't have a hitting coach in those years which was nuts. I don't know if Yogi was considered our hitting coach but I can tell you not once in all the years I was there Yogi never talked to me about hitting. I think people might have gone up to Ralph and asked him questions. I didn't do it."

"I would've loved to talk to him about hitting but I was so shy. I could play in front of 100,000 people and not feel anything but get me in a small room with a few people and a one-to-one conversation and I'm really shy. There were many times I would have loved to talk to him about hitting. Like I said, we had no hitting coach and if you were struggling you had to really work on this stuff on your own. I don't believe we had an indoor cage and we had to ask for extra batting practice. Looking back, I'm glad I had an opportunity to work with him those years and kind of pick his brain a little bit for some of his funny stories, and some of his not-so-funny stories. but I got a chance to get to know him a little bit. To this day I really wish that I would have had a chance or made the effort to talk to him about hitting and get his thoughts on hitting, maybe ask him for some help, again I just didn't do it for whatever reason. I knew I was well aware of his presence and what a terrific player he was and when he would come to the locker room I would always look at him and knew he was somebody special. Unless these guys were blind or didn't know anything about history, I think they felt the same way."

Shamsky said his favorite part of being on the show was getting to see Ralph Kiner's humility first hand.

"For me it was great. You were asked to be on it and it was usually a few minutes right after you got into the clubhouse. You didn't have time to sit back and think about the game, somebody would grab you right away. It was just a nice thrill. It was right down the hall from the locker room. You didn't have to go very far, you didn't have to go outside, and it was just nice. Ralph was kind of like a really down to earth guy. He wasn't this guy who graduated from college with these degrees in broadcasting and communications. He was a guy who played the game like you did but had this incredible career, particularly home run wise. His career was short. I think he only played ten years if I'm not mistaken. It was a short career in my eyes but he was such a big part of my youth growing up and I think that's important to understand that I was a big Cardinal fan growing up in St. Louis. I idolized the game, I idolized a lot of players who weren't playing for the Cardinals and he was one of them. He was one of those guys that I watched and idolized and he always seemed to be on a bad team, and was always leading the league in home runs. When you had a chance to be one on one with him and I always thought that was the key for me. Ralph's going to talk to me about something good I did but he's probably done something much better many more times than I did, so for me that was always a thrill."

"My favorite thing was that you sat down and were in a one-on-one conversation with Ralph. I don't think it gets any better than that. I mean, I hate to be redundant but this is somebody I idolized as a kid, and I felt that way with a lot of guys I played with and against. I saw them as kids growing up and got to play against them. I idolized guys like Mays and Aaron and Clemente and I got to play with some of the greatest players in the history of the game in the '60s and '70s. Even if someone else was on the show, his questions to you were directed to you and so for me that was always a thrill. I cherish those moments quite honestly, and I cherish those moments I had with him working with him as a broadcaster. "

For appearing on *Kiner's Korner*, Shamsky received the usual parting gift.

"Yeah, I think there might have been some gasoline coupons. I never received a physical gift like a watch or something like that."

Shamsky had the added privilege of working with Ralph Kiner in the broadcast booth when he joined the Mets TV broadcast team in 1980 and 1981.

"Well, when you say prepared, he knew the game. I don't think he was checking every stat of the guys he interviewed before the game. He relied on his own knowledge of the game, and he was a story teller. Somebody would hit the ball somewhere and it would remind him of a story, or someone would make a play and it would remind him of an experience. I think that was his greatest attribute. I don't think he was a stats and figures kind of guy. I mean he would look at the stat sheet, he would know some stuff, but he was really a guy who would tell the story of his own experiences. To me someone like that talking about something or telling a story, you have to listen because he was who he was. I think in '79, '80, those years I worked with him, he was tired, the game kind of wore him down. He got revitalized after the Mets started to get better in '84, '85, and of course '86, and then when [Tim]McCarver came over he was rejuvenated. I worked with him those years and the Mets were really a poor ball club. No matter what you said before the game you couldn't get people interested in watching; they just were not a good team and to his credit he would still tell stories and was so vibrant that I think he got rejuvenated. In the mid 80's, '84 and '85, the Mets started developing into a really good team and he was at the top of his game, but I still enjoyed those years with him and Bob Murphy. Those years were great for me."

Ron Taylor

August 17, 1969
Mets 3 Padres 2 @ Shea Stadium

From 1967 to 1971, Ron Taylor was a reliable right handed reliever for the Mets who saved a total of fifty games during that five-year period.

In 1969, Taylor went 9–4 and saved 13 games while tossing 5 2/3 scoreless innings in the post season for the World Championship team.

After his playing career, Taylor entered medical school and became a doctor. The Toronto native was the team physician for the Toronto Blue Jays. He was inducted into the Canadian Baseball Hall of Fame in 1985.

Taylor pitched two innings and ended the game by starting a 1–6-3 double play that first bounced off his head and earned him a place next to Kiner on *Kiner's Korner*.

"Well I was playing for the Mets and had just gotten hit with a line drive that bounced off my head. I picked up the ball and I threw it to second and then back to first and I got a double play out of it. After, Kiner showed me the tape and it was very funny. Now they take you off on a stretcher. He said

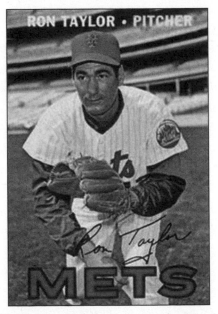

Ron Taylor: "How do you feel? You just got a double play off your head."
(Topps trading cards used courtesy of the Topps Company, Inc.)

'How do you feel? You just got a double play off your head.' Then I said 'Yeah, that was fun.'"

Before coming to the Mets, Taylor played for the St. Louis Cardinals and Houston Astros. As a visiting player he had never been on the show before, but he knew all about Ralph Kiner and *Kiner's Korner.*

"Oh yeah, besides being a baseball player, I was always a big baseball fan and I knew his career as a ballplayer. While I was with the Mets, we became friends and I have a great deal of respect for him."

After the game ended, Taylor said Ralph would be the one who personally invited him to come on.

"He would kind of wait for us to let us know that he wanted us to do the show and I said sure, I was always happy to do them."

Taylor felt comfortable with Kiner because he had been a player and could relate to one.

"It was great it was a big league program and I really enjoyed it. With a ballplayer doing the interviewing, you knew he was going to understand a lot. He was great. He respected all the players. The interviews were well prepared even though he only had a short time to do it, and he was just a real gentleman."

Taylor said Kiner did not have to tell everyone that he knew the game. His interviews and demeanor took care of that.

"He carried a great deal of knowledge about the game, and he was a great player himself. He did not flaunt this, he just did his job. Everyone appreciated that and was always ready to talk to him."

Ken Singleton

Sunday, June 13, 1971 @ Shea Stadium
Mets 5 Giants 4 (10 innings)

Ken Singleton grew up just outside of New York City in Mount Vernon, New York, and was drafted by the Mets with the third overall pick in the 1967 draft. The switch-hitting outfielder played his first two seasons with the Mets. Following a two-hit, three-RBI game, which he won with a walk off, sacrifice fly in the tenth inning, Singleton was asked to be a guest on *Kiner's Korner.*

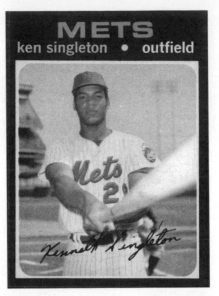

METS
ken singleton • outfield

Ken Singleton: "My dad had been watching *Kiner's Korner* all those years, too, and all of a sudden his son's on it."
(Topps trading cards used courtesy of the Topps Company, Inc.)

"I was only with the Mets for a year and a half. One reason I really remember going on because I used to watch Kiner's Korner *when I was a kid [growing up] in New York."*

"That was like one of the highlights of the day. Whenever it was a double header—those were the days when they had double headers—he [Kiner] would have somebody on inbetween games. I just thought as a kid growing up, this is a chance to hear the players speak. They didn't have all the interviews they have now, so Kiner's Korner *was a place where you could hear the Mets actually talk about that game that night or what was going on with the team at the time. I just thought that was really neat as a kid growing up watching* Kiner's Korner.*"*

As a fan of the show, Singleton knew all about Ralph Kiner as a Hall of Fame player.

"Oh yes, definitely. I knew that he was a great home run hitter. I think he led or tied the National League in home runs seven years in a row. I knew he was in the Hall of Fame. Of course I got to meet him when I was with the Mets. The Mets actually had him come down to an instructional league and kinda tutor me in hitting. I remember one day I hit a home

run in the game. I came back to the dugout and Ralph said, 'That's what I'm talkin' about.'"

Singleton was well aware that it was a big deal among the team to be asked to come on the show.

"Yeah, it was because that means you really had a good game. I know it was a sign of status when I came home that night. My dad had been watching Kiner's Korner *all those years, too, and all of a sudden his son's on it. It was a pretty big deal in our neighborhood."*

After watching the show many times, Singleton was now on the set as a guest.

"It was in a room off the tunnel, I remember that. It was in between both clubhouses at Shea Stadium. I thought it was really small. You don't get the real full effect on television but the set was kinda small. It was just big enough for two people and that's all they needed. It was one camera; that's all they needed. Of course Ralph would do the interview. I can remember Ralph interviewing the Mets of the early days like Roger Craig, Al Jackson, and Joe Christopher, guys like that. Charlie Neal, Choo Choo Coleman, all these guys, I remember those interviews. For me, to get on that show after watching it for so many years, I just thought, 'Man, you got it made, you're on Kiner's Korner. *How many little kids are watching you just like you used to watch this show?'"*

Singleton felt truly honored to be sitting next to Ralph Kiner who made him feel right at home.

"Of course he did. This is Ralph Kiner. First of all, he's a Hall of Famer and second of all he wanted me on the show and that means you've done something during the game. Ralph had all the questions. I was a young player in those days. It wasn't like I was an All-Star as of yet. I was just happy, maybe I was a little nervous, but Ralph had a way of making you feel at ease. Ralph wasn't really that new to me because I had been watching him all these years, so I kinda knew what the show was about. I don't know how long I was on. Eight to ten minute, whatever. It was over and I was on my way home. I was thinking to myself on the way home 'Man, I was just on Kiner's Korner'.*"*

Keith Hernandez mentioned that he received a $100 bill from Ralph when he went on the show. Did you get the same gift?

"I don't remember that 'cause it had been money long since gone. I knew there was probably a fee or some sort of prize you would get. That's the way the

shows usually are, but if it was a $100 bill I'm sure I accepted it. Whatever it was, it added to the thrill of being on the show for me."

Note from the Korner: in 1964, Philadelphia Phillies pitcher Jim Bunning pitched a perfect game against the Mets at Shea Stadium on Father's Day. Seven years later, Bunning would again start against the Mets on Father's Day. Singleton remembered that game.

"I was with the Mets in '71. Bunning pitched the Mets again on Father's Day [June 20] and my dad was at the game. I was in the big leagues by that time and I hit a long home run off Bunning. It went over the bullpen in right field at Shea Stadium. It was on Father's Day and my dad was there with like ten of his friends.

It was a big thrill for him. First of all his son was in the big leagues and he hit a home run on Father's Day with about ten of his co-workers there with him. The thing about it was when I was growing up he didn't get to see many of my Little League, Pony League, American Legion games because he was working. When he and my mom finally retired, they moved to Baltimore and the payoff was at the end because my last three years in the big leagues, they got to see just about every game."

Bobby Valentine

Monday, June 14, 1971 @ Shea Stadium
Dodgers 3 Mets 2

Bobby Valentine played parts of ten seasons in the Major Leagues and was a big league manager for three teams including the Mets from 1996 to 2002. Valentine is the Athletic Director at Sacred Heart University.

Valentine earned his appearance on *Kiner's Korner* after he slammed a two-run double that helped beat Tom Seaver and the Mets.

The native of Stamford, Connecticut, was well aware of the show.

"Being a local kid, yes, I was aware but I wasn't a Mets fan or anything. I have a somewhat vague recollection of a high school friend mimicking the star of the game in some of our Patriot league or high school games being on Kiner's Korner, *but I don't have a fresh recollection of watching the show itself. Fast forward to me actually being on the show and it was actually a bigger event then the at-bat."*

Bobby Valentine: "Being on the show and it was actually a bigger event then the at-bat."

(Topps trading cards used courtesy of the Topps Company, Inc.)

Valentine was brought to the iconic set of the show and it was eye opening.

"If I remember correctly the set was over in the Jets locker room. It was this makeshift studio, nothing like the bright lights, big sets that we know of today. I remember walking around a corner and the lights were on, I think there was like a partition in the Jets locker room. You walked in and you walked through the locker room and then around this corner and then this desk and really bright lights. I just really remember being amazed and I said this to Ralph hundreds of times. I just remember how humble he was. Here he was making himself just the post-game interviewer, not the great Hall of Famer that he was."

The show lasted less than twenty minutes but it made quite a lasting impact on a then twenty-one-year old third-baseman.

"It was big and somewhere in the hundreds of boxes of things that I have, I am pretty sure there is a small black and white photograph of me on Kiner's Korner *off of the television from either my brother's house or my aunt's house. My folks were at the game so they didn't see me on* Kiner's Korner. *Of course there weren't any recorders back then. The lasting memory was on my folks'*

mantle. This little black and white photograph of, I think, it was Jim Brewer, the relief pitcher who closed the game, who was a funny, funny interview, and a funny guy, and an older player and me, the young rookie, and Ralph. That photo was not there forever but it stayed there for quite a number of years."

Valentine knew it was kind of a big deal to be on the show and it also impressed his teammates.

"Absolutely. Not only because you were the star of that particular game, but remember unless you were from the area you never saw the show because you were always at the ballpark, and early on it wasn't shown in the club-house. There was no in-house feed, I don't even think the visiting clubhouse had televisions back then, so one of the major attractions of being on the show was that you got a gift. In those days it was a $50 gift certificate or I think there might even have been watches at one point or something like that, and the gifts escalated over the years. I think I got a $25 gift certificate for the best steak restaurant in New York City, that I never went to, but it was cool to get a $25 gift certificate because paychecks were hundreds of dollars for some and maybe thousands of dollars for others. No one was making a lot of money back then. It was one of the few shows that you would go on and you would actually walk away with something. That became as much of a draw as being interviewed by one of the great home run hitters of the game."

Even at a young age, Valentine was a "student of the game" and its history, so he was well versed in who the person conducting the interview was, although his teammates were not.

"You know, not really, not visiting players, not unless they were from Pittsburgh. I remember telling the guys I'm going on Kiner's Korner *with Ralph Kiner. I think it might have been Ron Cey or one of the young players in the clubhouse who dropped one of those 'Who's he?' on me. I played big shot because I knew everything about baseball history. Now remember, back then you had to read about it. You didn't turn on Sportscenter or MLB Network to find that stuff out. Guys were into their own careers. Most of the guys who were good were really into their own careers."*

The former Mets manager could not name his one favorite moment of being on the show but he did recall the host's words to him before the show began.

"I wish I could point to one shining moment, but turning the corner to the set, I still remember that first 'wow' of the lights and Ralph was kind

of sitting there writing some notes on a pad before he looked up and saw us coming. Then he complimented me on turning around [on] Tom Seaver's fastball and I always remembered that. He thought it was quite a feat for a young player to do that."

A huge hit off Hall of Famer Tom Seaver or being on *Kiner's Korner.* Which was the bigger thrill?

"It's not a slam dunk by any means because getting that hit was a big deal. It was off of Tom Seaver, and to allow Kiner's Korner *to even blow it out of proportion was a pretty special thing for me."*

Danny Frisella

June 19, 1971 @ Shea Stadium
Mets 6 Phillies 5 (15 innings)

Danny Frisella was a Mets relief pitcher during his six-year tenure. The right-hander made his debut in 1967 and had his best season in 1971 when he was 8–5 with 12 saves and a 1.99 ERA. Frisella pitched the final four innings of a 6–5, 15-inning win vs. the Phillies to earn a spot on *Kiner's Korner.*

Pam Frisella: "We would all go out to dinner on that fifty bucks, which just about paid for everything."
(Courtesy of Pam Frisella)

On New Year's Day 1977, Frisella tragically died from a dune buggy accident that occurred near his Phoenix, Arizona home. Danny's widow, Pam recalled that her late husband had been a guest with Ralph Kiner more than once.

"I didn't marry him 'til '71. I don't believe he was on it before that, because he didn't really make it up to the big leagues till mid-1970. He had to be on at least three because I remember how exciting it really was. You didn't know who was going to be on it until the end of the game. Generally whoever was on it, we would all hang out and all go out to dinner on that fifty bucks, which just about paid for everything, but I know he wasn't on it in '70, so '71 and '72 would be the dates."

Pam Frisella saw many of the games live at the ballpark so she didn't see Danny on the show on a television. Instead she was able to see the show live.

"I was watching it. I don't remember because it was forty years ago, I don't remember the type of studio it was or if we were sitting outside, I just remember watching it. I wouldn't be home to watch it so I watched it live."

Pam said Ralph Kiner was an important person in hers and Danny's life because of who he was and how he treated others.

"What I remember is [that] he treated the players with respect. In those days there weren't any big stars, maybe there was a Tom Seaver, but there wasn't a division of importance back then as there is now. There are the big players now, and it drops down. The Mets, in those years, they were all equal. I may be naive enough to think we are equal but I thought we were. I think we all supported each other. Nolan Ryan's wife had a reunion of all the first wives of the '69 Mets. She said she'll go to all these Old Timers' games and she won't know anyone because they would be second and third wives. So she had it at Texas Ranger's stadium. It was a tighter group of players back then. I felt we were equal."

During the season, Pam and Danny lived in a very friendly and cordial neighborhood.

"I still hear from our paper boy. After the internet went up, people started writing into the Mets data base to us. They washed our cars and waited for him. We were closer to the fans. We were just regular people. That's why I had fun."

When Danny Frisella was on the show, the neighbors would all be watching on WOR, Channel 9.

"I love how you say channel 9. He would come out and talk to those kids in the neighborhood. They would wait for him to leave and come home. We were only twenty-four so there was move of a connection between fans."

Pam Frisella said they were very appreciative of having Danny on the show because the gift of $50.00 went a long way in those days.

"Yep a $50.00 bill. I remember it because it was pretty exciting."

Wayne Garrett

Saturday, September 22, 1973 @ Shea Stadium
Mets 2 Pirates 0

Wednesday, September 29, 1976 @ Shea Stadium
Cardinals 7 Mets 2

On December 2, 1968, the Mets used the "Rule 5" draft to select third-baseman Wayne Garrett off the roster of the Atlanta Braves. By rule,

Wayne Garrett: "I never had a camera sticking right in my face before."
(New York Mets/Major League Baseball, via Wikimedia Commons)

Garrett had to remain on the roster for the entire season in 1969 and he played 124 games for the eventual World Champions.

In 1973, the Mets led a congested NL East by a half game over Pittsburgh with eight to play. The Montreal Expos, St. Louis Cardinals, and Chicago Cubs were within two and a half of the lead.

Garrett drove in the only two runs and southpaw Jon Matlack tossed a complete game, four-hitter as the Mets won an important game over the Cardinals 2–0. A nervous Wayne Garrett joined Hall of Famer Ralph Kiner on *Kiner's Korner* after the game.

"Yeah, I was nervous. I never had a camera sticking right in my face before. The camera was fairly close to you, and from what I remember it was only ten to fifteen feet away from you. I had never been in that situation before. Yeah, I was a little bit nervous."

"I knew that he was a good power hitter. I knew he hit a lot of home runs but I never saw him play."

Were you aware of the show before you appeared as a guest?

"I remember the show because we used to go in to the lounge and watch it after the game."

Garrett had a friendly relationship with Kiner, who traveled with the team, but always felt there was some distance between them.

"Well, Ralph was a good guy, a nice guy. He traveled with us. I was never around when he opened up. He could have opened up to other players. If he was opening up about his baseball career, I was never around at that time. He never related any of that to me. It's like the other two announcers, [Bob] Murphy and Lindsey [Nelson], they were more open. They were always friendly."

"Murphy talked to you all the time; he never walked by you without saying anything. Lindsey was like that too. Bob and Lindsey were more outgoing, Ralph was more reserved."

The left handed hitting third-baseman appreciated some hitting tips that he got from Kiner in the mid-1970s during spring training.

"It was sometime around 1974 or 1975. I went down to St. Petersburg in the off season because they wanted to make me a third string catcher. I remember Ralph being there for winter ball and we were in the cage talking about hitting. We also played golf. That's probably the closest I'd ever gotten to Ralph."

"Red" got something for his appearance but it wasn't extravagant. *"It might have been money or a dinner for two or a gift certificate."*

In July of 1976, Garrett was traded with Del Unser to the Montreal Expos for outfielders Jim Dwyer and Pepe Mangual. Later that season, Garrett would come back to haunt his old team as he hit a grand slam home run off Tom Seaver to power the Expos to a 7–2 win and an appearance on the show as a visiting player.

"We came back after I got traded and I hit a grand slam. I was hurt when I got over there."

Benny Ayala

Tuesday, August 27, 1974 @ Shea Stadium
Mets 4 Astros 2

Benny Ayala appeared in 45 games over two seasons as a member of the Mets.

On August 27, 1974, Ayala became the first New York Met to hit a home run in his first major league at-bat. That feat earned him a seat next to Ralph Kiner on *Kiner's Korner*.

Benny Ayala: *"Kiner's Korner,* it was a tradition."
(Courtesy of Benny Ayala)

At the time, Ayala did not speak English so he brought Felix Millan with him on the show to act as an interpreter.

"Ralph would ask a question then Felix would relay the question in Spanish, then I would answer it and Felix would tell Ralph in English. I was so nervous."

Despite the language barrier, Ayala knew that being on the show as a big deal.

"Yes, when I saw Tom Seaver and Cleon Jones in those days, they finish the ball game and then go inside to clubhouse and when someone came and got them for Kiners Korner, *they would always have a big smile on their faces."*

"I had heard about Kiner's Korner. *It was a tradition. For me he was a pioneer of that type of show after a ball game. I first heard of it in spring training. Ralph Kiner was my hitting instructor in the Instructional League. In those days the New York Mets and the St. Louis Cardinals had a partnership worked out at the same ball park and Ralph Kiner would take care of both the Cardinal and Mets players."*

Ayala, who knew Kiner as a great ballplayer, was amazed at Ralph's skills as a broadcaster.

"It was so impressive. I always looked at Ralph Kiner as a slugger, a super slugger, and here he was transforming himself into an announcer, with his own TV show. He was proud because he was no longer in that position of teaching me how to hit or anything like that. He was there to interview me after I hit a home run in my first game. It was like that with a lot of players because in those days all of the players would sit in the clubhouse and he would talk about hitting. He spoke about his approach to the game and some techniques on how to be a better hitter, a thinking hitter, not just to go up to the plate and waste time. He would sit in the middle and we would all sit there just like we were in a classroom but instead of being in school, we were in the clubhouse."

The Puerto Rican native said his experience on the show was a memorable one.

"The fact that I had the opportunity for a lot of people to look at me, the way I talked, the way I looked, the opportunity to let people know that I am there and a New York Met, and show my personality and get a little publicity off the field."

Not to mention the parting gift.

"I got a gift certificate to a restaurant near the airport."

Rusty Staub

Wednesday, April 23, 1975 @ Shea Stadium
Mets 7 Cardinals 1

Daniel Joseph "Rusty" Staub played in the major leagues for twenty-three years. Nine of those were with the New York Mets in two different stints. He was known "Le Grand Orange" in Montreal, but the Expos dealt the New Orleans, Louisiana, native to the Mets in exchange for Tim Foli, Mike Jorgensen, and Ken Singleton. Staub played a large role down the stretch of the 1973 season as the Mets rallied from ten and a half games behind in August to take over first place on September 21. Staub batted .307 in September with four home runs and sixteen runs batted in and finished the regular season with a fifteen-game hitting streak to help the Mets clinch the division on the final day of the regular season.

On April 23, 1975, Staub had one of his most memorable games in a Met uniform when he smacked a grand slam off of Hall of Famer Bob Gibson in a 7–1 win. The blow made a winner of Hall of Famer Tom Seaver and booked a seat for Staub next to Ralph Kiner on *Kiner's Korner*.

Rusty Staub: "You had a good game and more importantly you got fifty bucks."
(Mark Rosenman)

Staub said he enjoyed the times he sat down with Kiner.

"It was a big deal if you got to come into New York as an opposing team and go on Kiner's Korner. It meant that you had a good game and more importantly you got fifty bucks. It didn't get much better than that, coming from Houston and then Montreal, to get a chance to be on television in a big market like New York was also an added bonus. It gave you bragging rights in the clubhouse as well."

Staub said Kiner made you feel at ease.

"I knew how good of a player Ralph was and it was always great just sitting and talking with him. It was like two guys just having dinner. It was easy. It was a different era. You respected him as a ballplayer and he respected you."

Staub said despite the malaprops, he had ultimate respect for the man.

"I know that writers like to write about his missteps on air, and sometimes that became who he was, similarly to the 'Yogisms.' I prefer to remember him for the man and player he was. He was such a gentleman and I was fortunate to work with him as a broadcaster for ten years."

Jon Matlack

Wednesday, July 2, 1975 @ Shea Stadium
Mets 7 Cubs 2

Lefthander Jon Matlack was one game over .500 during his seven-year Mets career, but that won/lost record did not tell the whole story. Matlack was the 1972 National League Rookie of the Year and he helped the Mets to the 1973 National League pennant with a complete game, two-hit shutout of the Cincinnati Reds in Game Two of the NLCS.

On July 2, 1975, Matlack tossed a complete game win over the Cubs at Shea following the birth of his son earlier that afternoon. The big day was topped off with an appearance on *Kiner's Korner*.

"My wife was threatening the doctor with going on the road with us if he didn't induce her so he agreed. At 6 o'clock that morning we went to the hospital and somewhere around noon, my son was born and I was present, although I was not in the delivery room because I went to get lunch. When

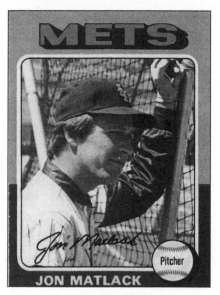
Jon Matlack was on *Kiner's Korner* the day his son was born.
(Topps trading cards used courtesy of The Topps Company, Inc.)

I came back they said, 'It's all over.' On the way to the ballpark, I picked up my cigars and passed them out to the guys in the clubhouse. I don't recall the score but I won the ballgame and go on Kiner's Korner, *and he's [Ralph] trying to talk about the ballgame and all I can talk about is my son being born."*

Do you remember who told you to go on, how you got the studio, and just how quickly everything happened after the game?

"Vague recollection of any of that. I couldn't tell you who might have been the person who made contact. After the first time, you pretty much know where the studio is and how to get there. It was right next to the locker room practically. From time to time I had used the camera control room to do charting because I could sit and watch the centerfield monitor. That made it easy to see pitch location, so I knew where to find it."

Matlack made numerous appearances on the show but didn't keep score.

"I honestly don't know if anybody 'kept score.' Maybe it wasn't a sign of status but something the guys looked forward to. I know I did. If the opportunity arose, I took it."

The southpaw pitcher was awestruck by the set.

"The thing that probably struck me more than anything else was the overall size from seeing it on television. It [was] a lot smaller and more inconspicuous then you might assume from seeing it on TV. The heat from the lights was something that jumped right out at you."

Matlack admitted that he did not really know about Kiner's career when he first got to the Mets.

"I was unaware until much later after my arrival that he had the type of career he had and put up those types of numbers. I came in as a pretty raw kid. I probably saw only four major league ball games in person before I actually played in one. I was more into playing the game and the competition than being a student of the game and being aware of its historic players."

In the 1970s, viewing video was not yet a staple in the sport but when players went on the show, Ralph would have video of the game. Was that helpful in preparing for your next start?

"I think absolutely it was unique. We acquired a yellow box on wheels that was a film apparatus. There was a guy who was hired to sit behind home plate and film the games so we could sit down and analyze them. The Mets were on the cutting edge but until it showed up, what you saw on Kiner's Korner was probably all you got to see of yourself other than still pictures."

Do you remember the gifts that you received?

"I guess the one that stands out the most, because I was a commuter, was the Getty gas certificates."

Del Unser

Tuesday, September 16, 1975 @ Shea Stadium
Mets 4 Expos 3 (18 innings)

In December 1974, the Mets completed a six-player deal with the Philadelphia Phillies that brought outfielder Del Unser to New York. (Catcher John Stearns and left-handed pitcher Mac Scarce were also acquired for outfielders Don Hahn, Dave Schneck, and popular relief pitcher Tug McGraw.) Unser played a season and a half in New York before being dealt to the Montreal Expos in 1976.

Unser's walk, with the bases loaded in the bottom of the 18th inning, drove in the winning run in the Mets 4–3 win. It also earned him a walk

Del Unser: "Ralph had an appreciation on how to play the game."
(Topps trading cards used courtesy of the Topps Company, Inc.)

onto the set of *Kiner's Korner*. The left hand-hitting outfielder batted .294 in 1975 and was well aware of Ralph Kiner's accomplishment during his career.

"Well, I think that was extremely high [respect for Ralph] given most Hall of Fame performers put up a lot of big numbers in a short period of time. Other than [Albert] Pujols, he put up the best numbers in his first five years than anyone else. I think if you knew anything about the game you were certainly aware of that."

The respect for Ralph was universal.

"Number one, he liked and respected the game and like a lot of superstars you don't really know how hard it is to play the game. I've spent a lot of time with Pete Rose and a lot of great players and sometimes they say, 'This is the way you hit to left field,' kind of like when Rod Carew says, 'Just hit it over there.' They weren't technical and they just do it. I think Ralph had an appreciation on how to play the game. From the time I was playing 'til now, I still scout for the Phillies. I've had a horrible time with names and remembering which name with which guy, but in terms of the names I remember them by the reports. I don't think Ralph had that gift nor certainly do I but it didn't take away from his knowledge of the game and how tough it is to play."

Unser was aware of Ralph's "Kinerisms," but it never took away from his respect for him.

"You know, I think he got mine pretty right at that point. I had seven years in the big leagues at that point. I wasn't a household name but I definitely got out there. I was very aware of his mispronunciations and the kidding he must have endured, but he was a beloved guy and everyone liked him."

Being around Ralph Kiner was always a pleasurable experience for Unser.

"I think the fans were waiting for him to mispronounce something. To me it was just another look that goes just beyond the game or a look into the person being interviewed. He may have mentioned my dad whom he may have played against or go more in depth about families or what have you. He would come up to you on the field and say 'Hi' or 'Nice going' on that road trip or something. Kinda make your day.

For being on the show, Unser got a free meal.

"Maybe back in '75 it was probably a certificate to a local restaurant

Yeah, it could have been to Joe's, the Chinese restaurant in Flushing where a lot of us went after day games."

Craig Swan

Wednesday, April 28, 1976 @ Shea Stadium
Mets 3 Braves 0

Pitcher Craig Swan was a 1972 third round pick who played his entire twelve-year career with the Mets, except for two games with the California Angels in 1984. In 1978, Swan led the National League with a 2.43 ERA and was second in walks plus hits per inning pitched (WHIP).

Swan earned a guest spot on *Kiner's Korner* following one of his best games as a Met. On April 28, 1976, Swan went the distance on a five-hit shutout while striking out eleven Atlanta Braves hitters.

Swan already knew about the show and was pleased to have been selected because it meant that he had a good game that day.

"Well I knew it because the players who did well always got to go on it, and they got a $50 gift certificate to Rusty's Restaurant in New York City. So that was big for us back then."

Craig Swan: "He was just the sweetest guy you could imagine."
(Topps trading cards used courtesy of The Topps Company, Inc.)

Swan remembered that he had an escort who took him to the set.

"Usually Arthur Richman [the Mets' director of publicity] would meet you at the door as you were coming in. If we only went seven or eight innings we'd be icing our arms so he'd come and get us in the training room and we would go down the hall."

Swan was taken aback at how small the set was.

"We were kind of jammed in that room and there was a little desk. Ralph was sitting at the end of the desk and there were usually two players if I remember. We were kind of jammed in there with that one camera, or maybe there were two."

In the early years of the show, many of the players saw themselves on videotape for the first time. When Swan joined Ralph, he had already seen himself on tape so it wasn't much of a surprise when it aired during the show.

"We did have a camera guy, Joey Fitzgerald. so we had tape of the game. Joey would sit behind the plate [filming] and I would work with the tape during the week. This way I could work on mechanics, or I could find something I actually did right just so I could copy it. So seeing myself on TV wasn't that big of a deal coming in from the game. We were just kind of used to it with all of the video."

Like many others, Swan knew all about Ralph Kiner's playing career.

"For guys to hit 50 home runs when he did that was quite a feat. He was also a member at Greenwich Country Club and I remember him well into his seventies still being able to hit the ball about 300 yards, so he had power right to the end. He was just the sweetest guy you could imagine."

Ralph Kiner's ability to relate to players made the sit down a memorable experience for Swan.

"One thing I liked about Ralph, because he was a hitter, I think when I would go in speaking about how to pitch hitters. You know certain pitches in certain counts. As a hitter he really identified with that so connecting that way with him was special.

He didn't bring up stuff that was negative. You never knew he was a Hall of Famer because he never said anything like that. He didn't lowball it, he just never threw it in your face. He never ever would come across like he was better than you in any way shape or form. I don't know, I just liked the way he would think of the game. He would remember parts and ask questions about specific parts. What pitch I threw, and how I got out of that inning. You know stuff like that."

Did Ralph ever mess up Swan's name with one of his Kinerisms?

"No he always got me right. He used to mix up [John] Milner and [Jon] Matlack all the time which was hilarious."

Jerry Koosman

Sunday, August 21, 1977 @ Shea Stadium
Reds 5 Mets 1

Jerry Koosman is considered one of the best left-handed pitchers in the history of the New York Mets. The Appleton, Minnesota, native won 140 games during his twelve-year tenure in New York.

Even though the Mets lost, "Kooz" was asked to be on *Kiner's Korner* with Reds winning pitcher Tom Seaver, who was making his first appearance against his old team for the first time since the infamous trade of June 15, 1977.

It wasn't Koosman's first time on the show, but the players never kept count of how many appearances anyone made.

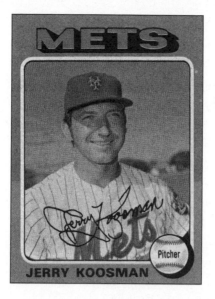

Jerry Koosman came clean on his Seaver-trade hoax on *Kiner's Korner*.
(*Topps trading cards used courtesy of The Topps Company, Inc.*)

"No, players didn't keep track. It was a nice little gesture to go on after the game. It wasn't intrusive on our time, it was fun to go on there. Ralph was a good friend of the team's and then you would get a little gift afterwards for it too. It didn't take long. You had just enough time before the show started to get ready, and it was kind of an honor to be asked to go on the show. It also meant that you did something in that game worthwhile of being on."

"I don't remember exactly who it was that would come down to ask if you would go on Kiner's Korner, *but the answer was always, 'yes.' I would go grab a beer and get my jacket on, then maybe you would have a minute or two and then off you'd go."*

Koosman recalled seeing the *Kiner's Korner* set for the first time.

"I was in the studio a lot before I was actually on the show. I would say hello to the guys who worked in there. When it was cold in the spring I would go in there to keep the pitching chart because you had a steady view of camera 4 which was the centerfield camera. I would just pull up a chair and I was always welcomed in there."

The Mets southpaw was familiar with Kiner's baseball career.

"Ralph had a Hall of Fame career and was inducted in 1975. He had been a Met announcer since day one. As a player you were aware of Ralph's

accomplishments in the game and how respected he was amongst the current players for his accomplishments in the game."

"Our team was more of a family. There were team functions that the announcers always attended. The announcers flew with us, and we knew them well. We got to spend a lot of time together whether it was on the plane, or at the hotel, or eating dinner at the hotel, so there were all kinds of conversations that took place. Kiner was always willing to talk with guys and help them out with hitting tips or just some great old baseball stories that you would learn something from."

All guests appearing on the show would receive a gift, but for Koosman, getting to be with Ralph was all that would matter.

"You know, I don't even remember anymore. I don't recall what the gifts were, I am thinking it was fifty bucks. To me it wasn't about the gifts. It was about going on with Ralph. It was always fun to be with Ralph Kiner. He made it such a relaxing show and you felt like you were at home in there."

After appearing multiple times, Koosman was asked what his favorite moment was.

"There were a lot of them, but the one that stands out in my mind is the first time I faced Tom Seaver after he was traded to the Reds. I lost that game 5–1, but Ralph had Tom and me both on Kiner's Korner *that night after the game. I was sitting next to Ralph and Tom was sitting next to me. Ralph opens up the show by saying, 'The two of you were teammates for such a long time, you must have some great times and stories about Tom that you can reminisce and share with us.*

I told a story [from 1975] about how I had purchased, from the back of one of the sporting magazines, this device that allowed you to broadcast over a FM frequency if you were within fifty feet of it. Tom always had a FM radio in his locker, it was the only music we had in the clubhouse, and so different guys would step on his stool and adjust the radio. The director, Jack Simon, did a great impression of Howard Cosell, so I planned this elaborate prank. At just the right time after batting practice when everyone was in the clubhouse, I had Jack go into the doctor's offices in the clubhouse which were real close to Tom's locker. Jack and I timed it out so I had time to get to Tom's locker and tune the radio to the proper frequency that, at the time, was 93.7. I go out and stand on Tom's stool and tune it in while Tom was talking to Mets chairman of the board M. Donald Grant just a couple of steps in front of his locker. They didn't think anything about me adjusting the radio because it was so common for us to do that, so a few seconds later Jack Simon as Howard Cosell comes blaring out of the radio, 'Hello everybody, this is Howard Cosell. We interrupt this program with an ABC Sports bulletin. The New York Mets have just announced a major trade. They have traded right handed pitcher Tom Seaver and left handed hitter Ed Kranepool to Houston for third baseman Doug Rader [who was hated by the Mets fans because of a fight he got into with Kevin Collins] and pitcher Doug Konieczny. (This guy couldn't get us out. Whenever they brought him in we just hammered him.)

The report is coming over Tom's radio nice and loud. Everyone in the locker room just stopped what they were doing to listen to this, then Jack as Howard Cosell says, 'And now we return you to your local stations.' M. Donald Grant takes off yelling what station was that as he is leaving the clubhouse. Seaver is stunned and dumbfounded. I walk over to Tom and hold my hand out to shake his hand to console him and wish him luck. I tell him I can't believe what I just heard, and he didn't want to raise his hand to shake my hand, so I just held it there. Finally he raised it and gives me a cold dead fish shake just grabbing on to the tip of my fingers. In the meantime Ed Kranepool was by his locker just 'm-f'ing' the Mets, throwing s**t in his locker. The entire locker room was in a turmoil. I see how serious this all was because they all felt, if it came over the radio, it had to be the truth. I run back and I tell Jack Simon to hurry up and get out of here and not to breathe a word of this to anyone.

We never said a word to nobody and this went on for years, so that night I am telling the clean version of this on Kiner's Korner. As I'm telling this on the show, Tom is sitting to my right. You can see on the monitors which camera shot they have of you, so when I am telling this they have a real tight close up of me. Tom leans in just out side of the camera shot and whispers in my ear just as I am nearing the end of the story 'You m***** f*****, you'. I laughed so hard. I mean, nobody had heard that story until that night and Seaver finally found out the truth about it. Without a doubt that was the greatest prank I ever pulled."

Kevin Kobel

Saturday, June 10, 1978 @ Shea Stadium
Giants 2 Mets 1

Kevin Kobel played six seasons in the major leagues, the final three with the New York Mets. The lefthander was 12–18 with a 3.58 ERA in a Mets uniform.

Kobel, who did not give up an earned run in six innings pitched, was the losing pitcher in a 2–1 decision to the San Francisco Giants, yet he was asked (along with winning pitcher Vida Blue) to be on *Kiner's Korner*.

"My first season I was 6–14. I was twenty years old, I had 24 starts and my era was under 4.00. I gave up less hits then innings pitched, so I understood struggling. One time I had three starts in AA [minor league affiliate level] where I hadn't given up an earned run and I was 1–2 in those 3 games, all 3 complete games by the way. It just seemed hard for me to win games. In that 1978 game, I had a real good start, which was my first as a Met. I went six innings and only gave up six hits and two unearned runs. It was my first start in the majors since 1974, and I felt I did my job the best that I could.

Kevin Kobel hid beers with Vida Blue on the *Korner*.
(Topps trading cards used courtesy of the Topps Company, Inc.)

That being said, I'm sure it's uncomfortable to be in that situation, but to be honest I was just so happy to be there. I got to meet Vida Blue and Ralph Kiner for the first time and be on the show. I lost but I always gave 100 percent so I was ok with it. I ran into Joe Torre a number of years later and one of the first things he said to me was that I was always one of his favorites, which showed me he respected how hard I played the game. So the short answer is, I was just happy to be there."

Kobel became aware of the show when he was promoted from the minors in May 1978.

"I didn't know anything about the show until I got called up from Tidewater in 1978. When I got to the Mets, it sounds funny, but the guys let me know about the show and said if you go on the show you get $50, so once you got to the Mets you knew all about it."

Even though the show was sponsored and produced by the Mets, appearances were limited in those days.

"Back in 1978 we did not have a very good ball club. If we had been better then maybe we would have been on more, but we only won 66 games and probably only half of those were at home."

After the game ended, how did Kobel know he was going to be on the show?

"To the best of my recollection one of the clubhouse guys or the club house manager who was Herb Norman at the time would come and tell you that they wanted you for Kiner's Korner. Usually I would be icing my arm, so I would have to go get cleaned up real quick. A lot of the players didn't shave on game day back then, so you could really tell who was picked to go on Kiner's Korner by who was by the mirror shaving and getting their hair just right."

Ralph Kiner had a real knack for making the guests feel comfortable, while also commanding respect.

"So that first time I was called to be on the show it was with Vida Blue. I don't think he knew what to do, and I know I didn't know what to do, so we just listen to Ralph. We sat down at the table and, like I said, I still really don't know what I am doing. After the game you're a little dehydrated and there was beer in the clubhouse. They don't have it there anymore because of the liability, but back then you would grab a beer, and it just so happened that day on the way up I grabbed a beer. When I get up there sure enough Vida's got one also, so when we go to sit down Ralph is telling us that we have

to hide the beers, that they can't be seen on camera, so we both said, 'Yes, sir,' and hid them behind the desk."

"Obviously, being in the Hall of Fame is something very special. Had I known earlier, human nature says I would have shown him even more respect. At the time he was in his sixties and he wasn't a very big man so to hear of what he did in Pittsburgh hitting all those home runs in such a short period of time was pretty amazing. I roomed with Robin Yount when I was with the Brewers and it's the same thing. We are all part of a fraternity and the guys that are in the upper echelon like Ralph and Robin earned the respect they get."

Ralph's reputation for reciting Kinerisms preceded him.

"You know there was a rumor that he would always mess up names, but he was such a professional. He was just such a humble man. I didn't even know at that point that he was in the Hall of Fame. I was there for two, two and a half years before I knew that. For someone to carry himself with such humility like that is a sign of a very special man. He worked hard at his job and was always so sincere. I never once heard him mess up."

For Kevin Kobel, the gift he received for being on the show was meaningful

"Absolutely, I remember. I got fifty dollars and I was thrilled. At the time I still had a place in Arizona and I was living in New York and it was very expensive, so with the amount of money I was making at the time, fifty dollars meant something to me."

Pat Zachry

Tuesday, July 4, 1978 @ Shea Stadium
First game of a doubleheader
Mets 4 Phillies 0

On June 15, 1977, a day that lived in Mets infamy—aka "the Midnight Massacre"—Pat Zachry became a New York Met as he was one of four Cincinnati Reds players who were traded for Hall of Famer Tom Seaver.

The right-handed Zachry pitched in parts of six seasons with the Mets. One of his best games came in the opener of a holiday twin bill as

Pat Zachary: "It was just an honor to be on the show."
(Mark Rosenman)

Zachry tossed a nifty, complete game, two-hitter in one hour and fifty three minutes.

The Mets lost the nitecap so Zachry was selected to be Ralph Kiner's guest on the show after the second game. Zachry said getting on a show like *Kiner's Korner* as a visiting player caught the attention of his teammates, not to mention the gift.

"No doubt, you bet it was, but you also have to remember that back then you had Mr. Kiner doing the show in New York. In Cincy we had Joe Nuxhall. Each city had people similar to Ralph's notoriety, so it was not that big of a deal as far as excitability because everybody had someone that was a big deal but it was New York and that added a bit to it."

"I think it was a gift certificate for a restaurant, which was just a ride from the ballpark which worked out just fine because it was on my way home. I think it was a steak house or an Italian restaurant. Either way, hell, there aren't too many bad restaurants in New York!"

Even though Zachry liked and respected Ralph, he did not want to discuss the controversial trade on the show.

"Well, the first thing I thought was, 'Oh my gosh, I didn't want to be there [in New York]. I had stayed six years in the minors for the Reds

and done well my first year. I had come off hernia surgery, so I was really angry about that as well. I didn't think I even needed the surgery. I was feeling fine and about two weeks from the end of the season we had our team physical and the doctor told me I had a hernia and they need to take care of it. I was fine and they said no we got to get this taken care of and you need surgery. Hell I didn't want to have surgery, but I had to have it done according to them, so I went ahead and did it and that put me back during the off season. I didn't get off to quite the start I wanted, and then they announced the trade which was quite a shock. It really took a long time to get over the trade and the physical set back of the hernia, so with all those feelings I sure as hell wasn't going to talk about them on Kiner's Korner. I was trying to be as much as a team person as possible even though I really didn't want to be there, not at first anyway. I think the biggest thing for me was being able to sit and talk with Joe Torre and the influence that he had on me as well as guys like [Jerry] Koosman, [Jon] Matlack, and Buddy Harrelson."

Zachry said Ralph Kiner understood the mentality of being a player, so that made it easy for him to relate to ballplayers of any era.

"He was respected by the players, not only for his playing ability but the way he carried himself. Ralph was a very gentlemanly person. He understood what you were trying to do, and what it took to get there. If he asked you for an interview or something and if you were just too busy or too tired, he was always like, 'Don't worry about it, we'll catch up next go round.' At the same time he understood what was going on so he knew when a good time to come back was. He was very workable with the players, he never forced himself on you. He never made anybody feel bad, which is one of the great things about him and Bob Murphy, they were both true gentlemen."

His favorite memory of *Kiner's Korner?*

"I don't think I could pick just one, it was just an honor to be on the show. It was probably the time I was pitching really well and made the All-Star team. I had put a nice string of wins together, of course, that was followed by one of the really bad moments when I kicked a helmet and broke my foot. There were some great ones as well with announcements of child birth and good things. It was just always an honor to be on with him as he was such a gentleman."

Lenny Randle

Tuesday, July 25, 1978 @ Shea Stadium
Mets 9 Reds 2

Lenny Randle played for the Mets in the 1978 and 1979 seasons. The versatile Randle manned numerous positions but he's best known for being the batter when the lights went out at Shea Stadium during the 1977 New York City blackout.

Randle keyed a five-run rally in the fourth inning with a two-run single to lead the Mets offense. Craig Swan tossed a complete game victory, but Randle was chosen to appear on *Kiner's Korner.*

"The legendary Arthur Richman would come down, and say 'hey you had great game, Ralph wants you for Kiner's Korner. *It's funny, if any of the other guys heard them tell you that, they would say 'Hey, bring me back a watch,' especially [Ed] Kranepool. He always wanted those watches. He must have at least ten of those watches or maybe he just sold them after the game. Then they walk you over to the studio."*

Randle knew all about Ralph Kiner from his collegiate days.

"Absolutely. It was because I went to college and went to Arizona State, where [former ASU coach] Bobby Winkles would talk about the greats of the game like Ted Williams. Hank Greenberg's son, Steve, was my roommate and

Lenny Randle: "It's Ralph friggin' Kiner!"
(Mark Rosenman)

when I was on the Olympic team with Ron Frazier, he would talk about Ralph Kiner. He called him one of the true power hitters to have ever played the game, and how he would get hit ten or twenty times a week and never flinched, just took the base or took you yard. To me that was a 'balls out' military guy, so I know all about him. Bill Mazeroski was also one of my coaches later on and he would tell me all about Ralph, so I when I got to New York I knew all about him and the show."

Randle was contemptuous that other players did not respect Kiner as a player.

"We actually had guys on our team that had no idea who he was, they were just in it for the watch. They would get three or four hits and were like 'Alright, I'm going to get a watch from Kiner.' I was thrilled to be around the guy because I respected him. Phil Caveretta would ask, 'Do you know who you are with?' and I would say, 'Of course, it's Ralph 'frigging' Kiner.' Pittsburgh Pirates, the balls out guy. I appreciated looking at him and his post-playing career plans. Lots of guys couldn't talk. He was articulate in a generation when some announcers were like 'Hi, I am Bill and I am a good player and I like to drink milk.' I mean, come on. Kiner was the total package, a real person, a speaker, a player, and a mentor. He was a role model, you just had to respect the guy. Willie Mays would tell me to go talk to Kiner, he was a legend to me."

"The guys of that era, had so much going on, not much different from today's technology. Like today's players they were selfish and they were not aware of who they could have learned from and be a sponge from and that's what separates a good player from a great player. The great players wanted to know from everybody, and Ralph was always open to us. If you wanted any help, any information, he had no ego, he was legit. He was never full of himself and a lot of players didn't know he was a Hall of Fame player. It's funny, the elderly get pushed aside in our society, so some younger players may have perceived him as just a wrinkled old guy doing an interview. They didn't take the time to appreciate the greatness or talk to him about it. They were more into the watch."

Randle's collegiate experiences helped him "break the ice" with Ralph.

"I remember walking in that first time and telling Ralph that 'Hank Greenberg says hi,' and Ralph was so surprised. He asked me, 'You know Hank?' I told him how Hank and his son Steve were my good buddies, so it

was a really good ice-breaker. To be truthful I was a little bit nervous, so I just wanted to get that out because I didn't know if I was ever going to be back on Kiner's Korner. "

The Mets' utility man impressed Kiner with his knowledge of the game.

"I used to have really good games against the Pirates, and Ralph would always ask me off the air, 'Why are you killing us?,' because he still had an allegiance to his old team even though he was a Met announcer and I could sense that. The Pirates had Bill Madlock and Bert Blyleven who were my friends and teammates in Texas, so we always had a private, friendly rivalry when we played against each other. Ralph would always ask, 'Why are you hitting like .488 against Pittsburgh?' I had no idea what I was hitting against each team, I was not a stat guy. I played the game, tried to get a hit and win the game. Ralph would always tell me how much the Pirates wanted me. Chuck Tanner was the manager at the time and Ralph told me that he really liked the way I played. I would always drop down a bunt because I knew it was one of Madlock's weaknesses, so we talked about that on the air. He asked me on the air, why I was such a student of the game?, and I explained that I studied players and their fielding abilities so I could get an advantage and get a hit. If I know I need a hit I can drop a bunt down between Tim Foli and Bill Madlock or Phil Garner if he was at third, or on the other side I knew that Willie Stargell had too much pasta. He was amazed and asked again about my studying of the pitchers and fielders, and I went on to tell him that based on the position of the infielders I knew instantly what type of pitch I was going to get and the location. This was way before defensive shifts and all. I knew that if the shortstop was playing me too far to the right of the bag and the third baseman was way back deep I know I'm getting a fastball in or a hanging curveball. If the shortstop is closer to the bag at second and the second baseman was shaded towards first I knew I was getting a fastball away. Ralph Kiner was so impressed with the fact that I was a rarity back then, a true student of the game, and would do anything to get on base, to this day is still one of my favorite moments. It's funny because all these years later the players still don't know. You have to have an IQ of about ten if you are Big Papi or Cano, although I think Cano finally got it. If the third baseman is playing at short and they have a shift on, bunt, it's a double,

I don't care about guts, or glory or ego, it's a double, or it's a single, you're on base. It doesn't matter if it's a screaming line drive or a bunt. A hit is a hit. Guys don't want to bunt anymore. I will never forget how impressed Ralph was with that conversation."

As far as the gift, Randle preferred the watch.

"Getty gas gift cards were great but, thinking back on it, gas was like 99 cents back then, so you would fill up your car, drive around and it was gone, but the watch was forever. It was a keepsake and if you did have the watch, it was special because it was a 'New York' watch from Kiner's Korner.

Doug Flynn

June 16, 1979 @ Shea Stadium
Mets 2 Braves 0

In his eleven-year career, second-baseman Doug Flynn hit a total of seven home runs, but it was one of those that landed him for a spot on *Kiner's Korner.* Flynn snapped a scoreless tie with a sixth inning home run off Atlanta Braves left-hander Mickey Mahler to lead the Mets to a 2–0 win.

Doug Flynn: "He made us all feel special."
(*Mark Rosenman*)

Flynn became a part of New York Mets lore when he was acquired from the Cincinnati Reds in the "Midnight Massacre" trade of Tom Seaver. He played parts of five seasons with the Mets and was a Gold Glove second-baseman in 1980.

The game ends and Flynn is asked to be on the show.

"If my memory serves me I would say Jay Horwitz [the Mets' media director] came and got me. Jay came and he would never tell you to go there. You know a lot of media guys would come and say, 'Hey, you need to be here.' Jay was always thoughtful of players. He'd say, 'Hey, would you mind going on?' and he was always very, very nice. I made it a point that whenever Jay asked me to do something I did it. So after the game was over you had a chance to go on and you just felt like well this is good because you did something good. Your team probably won the game or played halfway decent and here you get a chance and Jay asks you to go on there. It was never like, 'Aw heck, I guess I'll do Kiner's Korner *because you realized you were going to get a chance to sit down with a Hall of Famer, a great player, a guy who knew the game. He didn't always know you but he always knew the game. I wouldn't say you looked at it as an honor but it was something you enjoyed doing and you respected Ralph, and obviously you had a pretty decent game."*

Did you feel that being on the show was a sign of status within the clubhouse?

"I don't think anyone looked at it that way, but you figured that if you were on the show than you probably did something really good. If you came in 0–4 and booted a couple of groundballs, you didn't really expect to go on there."

Being on with Ralph Kiner was an eye-opening experience for the former second-baseman.

"No, I just thought it was pretty cool but everything for me at that time was pretty cool. Now you're playing every day, you're in the media market capital of the world and you go from five or ten reporters in your locker room to fifty. All of a sudden you get invited to go on television because we didn't have much TV, or as many TV games in Cincinnati. I don't think they had the TV package like they did in New York. You weren't really on TV except for Game of the Week *on Saturday, now you go to having televised games every time you step on the field. The audience knows you because of the opportunities*

to hear what the broadcasters had to say about you. Now you get a chance where you better hone your speaking skills. Of course, me coming with that brutal accent that I got, trying to remember words that I can say and can't say because there is so much slang. You know New Yorkers have their slang, Kentucky has [its] slang, so what I wanted to do was act like I was country but not like I was un-intelligent."

Flynn had the utmost respect for Kiner and tried to pass that down to players that came after him.

"He [Kiner] was by me. I don't know about all the other guys, I can't speak for them but I always had respect for the older players. That's why I used to enjoy all the Old Timers games. I would go out early, even when I was a player, and sit on the bench and talk to them. I tried to learn as much as I could from them and just listen to their stories. I always loved that. When I became a member of the old timers group and we would go and do Old Timers games, the players wouldn't even come out and watch us. They were inside doing their own thing on their computers and all that other junk. To me it was a sign of a lack of respect for the guys who had paved the way for them to make the kind of money they're making. That's why I appreciate the guys who will walk up to you and have respect for you. It didn't matter if you were a great player or not. Back in those days we were all in it together. We were all on strike together. We had all fought for the guys who were coming up behind us and the ones that had come before us so I thought a lot of guys in my era were like that. They had respect for the ones who came before us and I don't necessarily blame the guys who are coming up today for not having that."

Flynn admitted that his favorite part of *Kiner's Korner* was "waiting for Ralph to mess up somebody's name."

Flynn would seem like an easy name; did Ralph ever mess up yours?

"Mine wasn't too tough, but he would get confused a lot but that was the fun part of it. It was like listening to Dizzy Dean, or Yogi [Berra]. Ralph was such a great ball player that the thing that always really impressed me was that he didn't inject any of his own career into things he would talk to us about. You know he never said, 'I can remember when blah, blah, blah'. He would never do that. He would try to do the interviews as straight as he could and let us be the stars. I always appreciated that. You know with the numbers that he put up for so many years and how great he was, he never really tried to

hang that over anybody's head. He said you guys are on the show, I'm just the guy doing the broadcast. You are the stars, and he was very good about letting us do that. I was very appreciative of those times. He tried to make you look special. He would always be very complimentary, he wouldn't go on about, 'Well, you're struggling through the season'. He didn't really dwell on the negative, he tried to highlight the positive. As you know everybody is trying to look for a different angle, but he didn't do that. I don't know if he will go down in history as the greatest broadcaster ever, Probably not. For those of us who got a chance to be interviewed by him we will certainly have respect for him, not only as a great player, but because he made us all feel special."

Flynn was one player who really didn't care about the gift he would receive.

"I used to give them all away. If I was lucky enough to go on there I would give them away to the clubhouse guys or Jay [Horwitz] or somebody. It wasn't much but it was more just a token. You know going on that show was fun because it was always fun to go on with somebody. It was always fun to go on and feed off them. I'm not too serious. I'm always playing stuff off and trying to have a good time. You know baseball was fun and probably could've been a whole lot more fun. I wanted to go on because I thought it was entertaining, you know let's go on and entertain the folks. You've seen my act before, you know how it works."

Pete Falcone

Monday, June 25, 1979 @ Shea Stadium
Mets 4 Pirates 0 (second game of a twi-night doubleheader)

Pete Falcone grew up in Brooklyn, attended the same high school as Sandy Koufax, and pitched for a New York team. The southpaw was dealt from the Cardinals to the New York Mets in time for the 1979 season. Falcone pitched four seasons in his home town but on this Monday night in June, he tossed a complete game, five-hit shutout. It was clearly his best game as Met and it earned him a seat next to Ralph Kiner. Having grown up in New York, Falcone knew all about the show.

"Of course, I grew up in Brooklyn and New York City and I even grew up in parts of Long Island. Growing up I was a Yankee fan quite honestly,

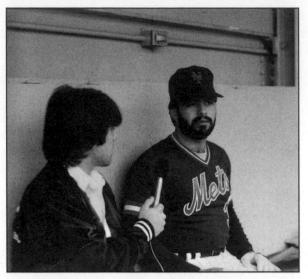

Pete Falcone: "I always watched *Kiner's Korner*."
(Mark Rosenman)

even when the Yankees folded up in the mid 1960s after Mickey Mantle and the stars started to decline. It was a rough time to be a Yankee fan from 1966–1969, so I also watched the Mets. I always watched Kiner's Korner. *You had to watch it if you watched a Met game. It was on after every home game and it was such a good show you looked forward to it."*

Falcone threw the last pitch of his gem and then was summoned to the show.

"If you were a Met or a visiting player, right after you had a great game at Shea, a kid would come down into the clubhouse and tell you that Ralph wants you on Kiner's Korner. *You would go over to the studio and if it were a really warm night, you would actually still be sweating. You didn't have time to take a shower, you were on immediately after the game. The game would end, the announcers would do a real quick recap, go to commercial and then right to* Kiner's Korner. *I know a lot of guys went in there with their uniforms on and they were dirty, but they would basically walk in, sit down, wipe the sweat off their face and talk about the game."*

"I remember pitching good games against the Mets, but I was never ever able to get a win, so it wasn't until I became a Met that I got to go on Kiner's Korner. *We never kept track but it was a big deal. I remember teammates of mine on the Giants and Cardinals going on there and it was a big deal."*

The Mets lefty had seen the show on TV, but didn't realize what went into it until his appearance.

"It was really low-key. It was only Ralph, a couple of camera guys and a couple of other people in the room. You had a Met logo in the background and a paneled wall and a few chairs, maybe enough for two or three people, and you would just sit down and Ralph had done it so many times, it was nothing to him, it was like ho-hum. He would recap the game, and it was just like two guys talking. You weren't even aware of the camera. Even though you were looking into the camera and you knew you were on television, he kept everything low key so you were never nervous."

Falcone was one who knew about Kiner's on-field achievements.

"Ralph was a home run hitter. People don't realize he hit over fifty home runs in a season twice in his career. He played for a perennial last place team with Pittsburgh in the 1950s. The Pirates were just horrible, and he was hitting home runs for that team. By the time I met Ralph he was an older distinguished gentleman. He always was dapper. He dressed well, spoke well, and just carried himself so professionally, and all the guys had tremendous respect for him. We all knew he was a legitimate dominant power hitter in his day. I remember him telling us a story about how he led the league in home runs in 1952 and his team lost 112 games. The GM at the time was Branch Rickey and he cut Ralph's salary. Ralph went in and argued that he was the most valuable player on the team but Rickey told him, 'We can lose 112 games and finish last without you.'"

Was it cash, or a watch or something else that he received as a gift for appearing on the show?

"I know I never got a watch, I know it was never cash, and I honestly don't remember but I am thinking maybe it was a gift certificate to a restaurant."

The game became more memorable for Falcone because he got to go on the show.

"Not too many pitchers had complete game shutouts against that team [Pittsburgh] that went onto to win the World Series. Back in those days unfortunately we were a really bad ball club. You look back at our records and we were the punching bag of the league, so many times it was the opposing team's guys going on Kiner's Korner instead of the Mets. When you won a game for those Mets teams, you sat back and thought wow, so getting my first win as a Met and then going on the show would have to be my favorite moment."

Steve Henderson

Saturday, June 14, 1980 @ Shea Stadium
Mets 7 Giants 6

In the history of the New York Mets, Steve Henderson is known as one of the players who was acquired in the "Midnight Massacre" trade for Tom Seaver. Henderson played twelve years in the majors, four with the Mets.

"Hendu" had his Mets moment on September 14, 1980, when he slammed a walk off, three-run home run off of Giants right-hander Allen Ripley to cap a five-run rally and clinch a spot on *Kiner's Korner*. Giants pitcher John Montefusco was originally scheduled to be the guest until the Mets staged their rally.

Henderson did not know much about the show when he entered the studio to sit down with Ralph for the first time.

"No, not really. I had heard a little bit about it, I hadn't known what it was about, but before the year was over, I was on there a lot."

After he touched home plate, "Hendu" got the word that he was chosen to be Ralph's guest.

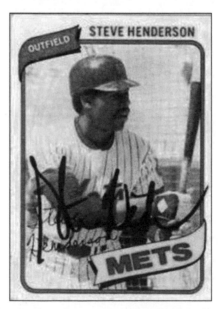

The Schaefer Beer Company was thrilled with the exposure they got from Steve Henderson.
(Mark Rosenman)

"Well, the clubhouse guys would let you know that the people from Kiner's Korner were looking for you. The producer would come and get you way before you had a chance to sit down, and they would bring you to the studio which was right when you came out of the dugout. You would make a right and then it was a couple of doors down on the right hand side, that's something I will never forget."

Henderson was understandably nervous about his initial appearance on the show.

"To be honest, I was a little scared. I'm in the big leagues and now all of a sudden it was different. We had some reporters when I was with the Reds in the minors but now I was about to have everyone in New York looking at me, but again Ralph had a way of relaxing you, joking with you, and doing a good interview, which helped a lot."

Henderson was so impressed with the host that he went and did some research on the Hall of Famer.

"At the time I didn't know anything, but I then went and read some things about him. I came to know how good a player he was with the Pirates, and was amazed at how most of the players knew all about him. For me I always respected the guys who came before me. I have always done that, and I try not to change that, and that's why out of respect for him, I did my research on him, and I continue to do that today as well."

Teammates would take note of who would go on the show after a win.

"Without a doubt, we kept track, even though those teams were not that good, we always looked forward to going on Kiner's Korner. Mr. Kiner was such a good guy, I mean he never ever tried to embarrass you or anything. He was always very honest with you, he always asked real good questions, I thought he did a really good job."

Was there ever any jealousy over who was chosen?

"No, not at all. Even though those Met teams didn't play as well as we wanted to, we were really good teammates. Maybe some of them got tired of seeing me go on so much because I just got lucky a lot of times in some of those wins we had."

The parting gifts were a topic of discussion in the clubhouse.

"During my days it was Getty gas gift cards. I had so many of them back then it was great. I also used to wear a t-shirt on the show, a Schaefer beer *shirt. It was kind of a good luck shirt, and I think the people at Schaefer beer saw it, and they sent a clubhouse guy to me and told me they would send me anything I want for wearing it. I thought at first they were just joking so I said, 'Ok, send me four or five cases of beer.' The next day there it was right by my locker. Five cases of Schaefer beer. I wound up shipping them to my dad in Houston, but it was great. I just had that Schaefer shirt on for good luck. I always got a lot of hits whenever I wore it. I didn't know anything about advertising then, so as long as I was getting hits I was going to keep on wearing that t-shirt."*

"Hendu" made a couple of appearances on the show but his favorite moment was his first.

"It would have to be the June 14, 1980, game when I had the walk-off, because it was also the day I got engaged. I hadn't hit a home run yet that season. I had given her the engagement ring at the airport and then the next thing I know I hit the game winning home run and then I'm on Kiner's Korner. *It was really a pretty exciting day."*

Ellis Valentine

Monday, May 3, 1982 @ Shea Stadium
Mets 10 Braves 4

Three hundred sixty-seven days after he was acquired from the Montreal Expos for reliever Jeff Reardon and outfielder Dan Norman, Ellis Valentine earned a spot on *Kiner's Korner* after his only four-hit game with the Mets.

Valentine was a former All-Star who was making his second appearance on the show. He previously sat down with Ralph as a member of the Montreal Expos in 1977 following a two-run home run off of Mets pitcher Jerry Koosman that keyed a 3–2 win.

"I just remember going on the show, him [Ralph] being so gracious. It was quick, you know? You were in you were out, but he praised you for the game and your excellence and what took place. There was never any shaming or political attacking or anything like that. He was always a class act."

Valentine appreciated his time with Ralph Kiner.

Ellis Valentine: "It was just a given, it was going to be done right."
(Mark Rosenman)

"It was just a feeling of joy that you were being recognized for something, and you know its Ralph Kiner. He [was] no joke himself. It was just a pleasure. After a while I did it and I may have taken it for granted but after a while I'm kind of stroking myself saying that I've been on there several times. It was always comfortable, it was very nice, and it was well done. It didn't take up a whole lot of your time you know a lot of us were party animals back in the day, and we wanted to get out of there and go party. He didn't keep you long. You know, he hit it and got you out of there."

Valentine said the respect for Ralph was overwhelming.

"I don't know if everyone knew how great he was, but we all knew he was respected. I knew of him through others who had a personal relationship with him. He was just a decent man, and a good man to the players. There was never a feeling of challenge or threat coming from him to a player. It was always a good safe time to spend with Ralph."

Valentine's favorite part of being with Ralph was sitting down with the man.

"I just liked being there. I think being there was a pleasure in general. I just don't remember it being anything other than just being there with Kiner. It was just a joy to be in there with him, go and get your moment. He just handled you with class every time. It was just a given, it was going to be done right."

Valentine, who went to Crenshaw High School in Los Angeles, (as Darryl Strawberry had), said the gift was trivial.

"Yeah, he gave me a '53 Chevy once, no I'm just kidding. It was a $50 bill."

Ricky Horton

Monday, April 14, 1986 @ Shea Stadium
Cardinals 6 Mets 2

Lefthander Ricky Horton pitched for three teams (the White Sox, Dodgers, and Cardinals for two different stints) during a major-league career that lasted from 1984 to 1990. Horton appeared in three World Series, in 1985 and 1987 with St. Louis and 1988 as a member of the Los Angeles Dodgers. He is currently a broadcaster on Cardinals telecasts on Fox Sports Midwest.

The southpaw grew up ninety miles north of New York City in Hyde Park and followed the Mets by watching games on WOR-TV.

"Growing up, we were able to watch WOR TV, and we got the Yankees too, so we had both growing up. I was more of a Mets fan, and interestingly all of my extended family were either Met fans or Cardinal fans. My grandmother was kind of the matriarch of the family. She lived in Poughkeepsie, New York. I lived in Hyde Park which was nearby, but she had this great influence on our family. She had seen Stan Musial play when she was younger and she took my uncle to see "Stan the Man" play so he became a Cardinal Fan, because Musial was just such a great representative of baseball.

She was this tremendous influence on our family and because of that all of our family was either Cardinal or Met fans. When I would go to games as a kid, we would drive down to New York and only go to see Cardinal-Met games. Growing up, I watched some of the Cardinals players like Mike Shannon, who I got the chance to work with, Bob Gibson and all those guys, but I was a Met fan. Even though my grandmother wasn't too happy about that, when I was drafted by St. Louis, it was a neat family thing for me, but I still had that New York Met connection in me."

Horton not only followed the Mets, he also got hooked on *Kiner's Korner.*

"Watching the games was one thing, but I had every Mets player up on my wall. My favorite player was Ron Swoboda, so I am going back to the late 60s and remember 1969 very well. My mom let me stay home from school and I watched Ron Swoboda make that diving catch in the World Series (in Game 4), so Swoboda was my favorite player. I still have that baseball card. The guys that I followed in my formative years were [Ed] Kranepool, [Tom] Seaver, [Jerry] Koosman, Tommie Agee, Cleon Jones, and Jerry Grote. Those were guys that I just lived and died with, so I watched Kiner's Korner after every game. I vividly remember Bud Harrelson, Cleon Jones, and Tom Seaver talking about the game and I would imagine myself someday getting a chance to do that. I remember when Seaver was on Kiner's Korner, and when Ralph asked him about an exercise or things he did to get stronger as a pitcher, Tom talked about tying a weight to a wooden dowel with a string and rolling the weight up and down and then back up and then back down to build up strength in your hands and wrists. I did that because Tom Seaver said it on Kiner's Korner. As a kid I was hanging on every word, but I really pictured myself not just being the star of a really big game, but being on that show to culminate it and talk about it as it truly was a dream of mine."

Horton started the Opening Day game against the Mets on April 14, 1986. The lefthander tossed 7 innings, giving up a run on two hits but he got a no-decision.

Horton thought he was a prime candidate for a guest spot on *Kiner's Korner*, something that he thought about doing as a youngster.

"I go into the clubhouse and I am pretty elated. I had just pitched against Dwight Gooden who was just the best pitcher you could imagine at that time. I still have such tremendous respect for Dwight, and always loved being around him, so I was pretty amped up about the game I just threw. The minute I get into the locker room, Mike Shannon [Cardinals radio broadcaster] calls me over and wants me for the "Star of the Game" interview for the Cardinals Radio Broadcast, so obviously I am not going to say no to that. While I am doing the radio interview, evidently someone was looking for me to be on Kiner's Korner. No one really knew that being on that show was kind of a dream of mine since I was a kid, so here I am with Shannon, doing the radio spot and it's a long interview. By the time it was done I remember the clubhouse guy said, "Yeah they were looking for you for

Kiner's Korner *and couldn't find you." It was like so deflating for me, like yeah I may have just pitched well against Dwight Gooden but what I really wanted to do was be on* Kiner's Korner. *What I also remember about that day was after the game I drove back home to Hyde Park with Andy Van Slyke, another former New Yorker, and we talked about the game on the way home. It was a big game, the Mets home opener. Even though I did lots of interviews after the game, on the ride home I kept thinking as awesome as this day was I still missed out on something that mattered to me in a way people quite did not understand."*

Cardinals shortstop and Hall of Famer Ozzie Smith had three hits and drove in two runs to power the offense that day. When the show could not get Horton, they "settled" for Smith.

The lefthander was disappointed because there was a prevailing sentiment amongst the players in those days.

"I certainly had my feelings on it, but it was understood that this was the show to be on. They treated you better, and it was a much bigger deal. It wasn't just a post-game interview. This was a real show at a time when there weren't a lot of postgame shows on. It's funny because I actually do postgames for the Cardinals now which is so ironic because not only do I work games on radio and TV, but I've done postgames and pregames for the last ten years or so. I get to do my own version of it, but going into New York, you knew that was just a different place, it was a much bigger show, a much bigger experience."

Many players only knew Ralph Kiner on TV, but failed to realize that he had a Hall-of-Fame career as a player.

"I don't know if they knew it to the level that I knew it. I knew so much about him. His first few years no one had better numbers. His name came up a lot on Cardinal telecasts because when Albert Pujols was putting up numbers early in his career, we were stating that only Ralph Kiner hit more home runs (215) in his first five seasons than Albert (2001–2005). In some ways, Ralph was an unsung hero and maybe remembered more so as a broadcaster than a player, but the truth is, he was a great player."

Memorable moments were a staple of *Kiner's Korner*. Horton reflected back on one of those moments.

"In 1987, Tim McCarver once approached me on the field and said, 'Hey, I heard you didn't get a chance to be on Kiner's Korner *last season. We*

heard you really wanted to be on, but I'll tell you what, we want you to do the intro to Kiners Korner, so we will tape right here on the field.' McCarver brought a camera crew onto the field of Busch Stadium and we recorded something as an intro to Kiner's Korner for the next show. I am so grateful to Tim for that. I can always say I was on Kiner's Korner, which was a 'bucket list' dream fulfilled."

Tim Teufel

Monday, April 21, 1986 @ Shea Stadium
Mets 6 Pirates 5

Tim Teufel grew up in Greenwich, Connecticut, so he knew all about *Kiner's Korner.*

"I was a Yankee fan growing up as a kid, but I would flip on a game and watch the Mets broadcast on WOR as well, so I knew all about Lindsey Nelson, Bob Murphy, and Ralph Kiner and Kiner's Korner. My first real introduction to it was when I watched it on TV as a kid, my next introduction after that was live. When I got traded over from Minnesota to the Mets, Jay Horwitz was the Mets' PR guy; in fact, he is still there now. He would

Tim Teufel (right): "He just made you relax instantly."
(Mark Rosenman)

prep all the new players that came to the Mets for a show like Kiner's Korner, *and how to do interviews with the media.*

Teufel joined the Mets for the 1986 season and in his sixth game, he delivered a two out, game tying double in the bottom of the ninth and then scored the winning run to earn a spot on *Kiner's Korner.*

"It was one of those situations where when you came in to the clubhouse, they would tell you Ralph wants you for Kiner's Korner *and the network wants you on there. You had time to get in there, it was ample time. You had a chance to change your shirt or maybe throw on your pullover, and then they hook you up with the mics, it was a big deal. They walk you through everything as well. They tell which cameras to look at, and Ralph of course makes you feel so comfortable. He was such at pro at it; he has been on both sides of it so as a professional announcer it was nothing to him. He just asked me the questions and most of them were easy to answer. He was in that realm for so long, he made it so easy on the players with nice 'lay up' questions and we tool it from there."*

Having watched the show on television, Teufel had some idea of what to expect but it was still eye-opening when he made his first appearance.

"You knew it was something special. This was a 'one on one' in a studio with a camera so you knew a lot of people were watching. It was a little more attention on you, it was an attention-getter as well, so you walked in and Ralph's a pro. He is all ready to go. He says, 'Hey Tim, you had a great game, this is what we are probably going to talk about. That was nice that you got that base hit to right field to drive in that run.' He just made you relax instantly. Plus, it was just so well done, it was relaxed, it was easy, no stress. It was like you were talking at the kitchen table about the game after it all happened. When the lights came on all of a sudden you get the sweaty palms going and you realize the magnitude of wanting to sound and look right when you are going out over the air live like that."

"Ralph was well respected. We all knew he was a home run hitter. We knew he was a serious player with Pittsburgh for many years. He was very fair behind the mic, and he also did it as a player. He was just a class guy so you respected a guy like that. You never looked at him as an announcer. You looked at him like a Hall of Famer."

Like many before him, Teufel's appearance on the show meant that he had done something in the game.

"If you were on Kiner's Korner *you had a good game or you did something significant that warranted it. They just didn't bring anybody on. It was usually the guy who did something good for the team, and it was always kind of neat to be asked to be on."*

When it was over, Teufel had a sense of, "That wasn't so bad."

"You walk in there with a feeling of, 'Ok, what's going to happen here?' and in the end you kind of remember how uneventful the event actually was, because it was relaxing. It happened so quickly. Six, seven questions and you're done and the show is over. It wasn't something you had to sit there for an hour. All of a sudden you are in front of the cameras and then it's over in a flash. You hear Ralph say, 'Thanks, Tim, for coming in and here's your parting gift.' It's all over and you're walking down the hallway thinking 'Wow, that wasn't so bad.'"

And the parting gift was?

"I usually got a watch, the old 'Armitron' or a 'Citizen,' something like that. I would give them away, to my dad or whoever needed a watch."

Ed Hearn

Sunday, June 15, 1986 @ Shea Stadium
Mets 8 Pirates 5 (2nd game of DH)

Ed Hearn had a modest, three-year big league career. His first year in the majors was 1986 when he was the backup catcher for the team that won the World Series. Hearn is probably best known for being one of the players who was traded to Kansas City in exchange for pitcher David Cone.

On June 15, 1986, Hearn hit his first major league homerun and drove in three to lead the Mets to a sweep of the twin bill against the Pirates. After the game, Hearn earned a guest spot on *Kiner's Korner*.

"I'm a player in New York in my rookie year and it's that championship year for the Mets. I was trying hard to fit in. In the minors you might get a game on the radio and I remember thinking wow we may have a couple of thousand people listening to everything that is going on in this game. I get to the Mets, which is probably one of the only markets at that time that had every single game televised, so that first week you're like, 'Wow, there are

cameras everywhere.' I was afraid to even pick my nose for fear it would be on TV, and then I heard about Kiner's Korner. *Guys would be on-one-on one after the game. So I remembering hearing about it in the clubhouse before I ever got a chance to be on."*

Hearn's appearance on the show did not set in until he got to the set.

"It was like, 'Wow, this is big time.' I still got a sweat going, because it always happened pretty quickly after the game. You're still in your uniform, you take a seat, and I just kept thinking, 'Oh, so this is how it all works.' You just take it all in, and then Ralph turns on when the camera turns on—well, as much as Ralph turned on, that is. This was my first taste of a real postgame show. It was like, 'So this is what it is like to be a professional baseball player'. It is big, bright and shiny in New York."

Hearn did not realize what kind of player Ralph Kiner had been until after he appeared on the show.

"It occurred to me what a real shame it is, that we get caught up in the fast pace of our lives and we miss out on so much. I never got to know Ralph Kiner. Never just sat down and talked with him. He was there with us on road trips and around the park all the time. If only I had just taken the time to communicate with him. He was a Hall of Famer, and for some reason I didn't respect that enough back then. I never thought of him like Willie Mays or Babe Ruth. When I look at his stats now and see he hit home runs I realized he is a true Hall of Famer. When I read articles such as one by Marty Noble where Marty called him [a] 'genuine and most charming gentlemen' that saddens me because that's exactly the type of person I would have loved to get to know and I missed out on that opportunity. All I thought about him back then was that he liked to drink a little and messed up people's names. We really didn't talk much about Ralph in the locker room; it was more about Fran Healy who was kind of an Ed Hearn type of player, and Tim McCarver. It seemed we all knew Tim, because you just can't help it. Tim was real flamboyant whereas Ralph was kind of reclusive to me."

Ralph's endearing penchant for getting names wrong provided Hearn with his favorite moment of being a guest on the show.

"The fact that throughout the interview he kept calling me 'Sid,' and the realization that on my best day of my career I was going to be known as 'Sid.' The great part of that day was it was Father's Day. My parents were at the ballpark. There are some pictures of me pointing at my parents in the

stands, which is totally out of character for me, as I'm headed to the dugout after the home run, which was also my first home run in the big leagues. It was such a thrill because it was at Shea, so it became my first curtain call. I was raised to be humble, never show anybody up, even though now I wish I was a little more like [Len] Dykstra and [Wally] Backman. I was raised to be very conservative and be respectful, but when I get to the dugout [Keith] Hernandez and [Gary] Carter are pushing me to get my ass out on the dugout steps to take a curtain call. That ends up being the cover of my book, me standing on the steps with my finger in the air. Hell, I didn't know what to do, and the whole time I am thinking this is not me. As I am being pushed up the 'dang' steps and Shea is rocking, it might have been good for Kid [Gary Carter], because Kid would love to get up and be in the camera and all that but that just wasn't Ed Hearn. One of the ground's crew guys had retrieved the home run ball. I am sure he had to trade a bat or something for it, because it was such a big valuable thing after all, an Ed Hearn Home run ball. It may have cost him fourteen Gary Carter bats or something, but they got the ball, so after Kiner's Korner *I was able to give the ball to my dad on Father's Day. So all around it was one of my most memorable days as a pro."*

. . . .and the gift?

"It was an Arbitron watch."

Keith Hernandez

Wednesday, September 17, 1986
Mets 4 Cubs 2 (Mets clinch NL East)

On June 15, 1983, the New York Mets completed a deal with the St. Louis Cardinals to acquire the best first baseman in the history of the franchise.

Keith Hernandez was a National League Most Valuable Player and an eleven-time Gold Glove winner who became the spiritual leader of the team. "Mex" would play seven years for the Mets and would help lead the team to a World Series championship in 1986.

Hernandez appeared on *Kiner's Korner* as both a Cardinal and a Met. As a student of the game, he knew all about Ralph Kiner the player.

Keith Hernandez: "I can't wait. I hope I can get on that show."
(By slgckgc, via Wikimedia Commons)

"I knew about his career, absolutely, but I did not know Ralph other than, 'Hi, how are you?', because we [The Cardinals and Mets] shared the spring training sites [St Petersburg, Florida] back in those days. I didn't know whether to shake his hand. He wasn't one of those guys that sought you out, he wasn't chatty."

Like many others, Hernandez had known all about *Kiner's Korner*.

"Oh yeah, it was always on after the game in the clubhouse [in both the home and visitors' rooms]. I remember thinking, 'I can't wait, I hope I can get on that show."

What was your first impression when you got to the set?

"It was nice to meet Ralph. I knew all about him. Of course, you got your $100 bill. I remember looking at the monitors on the camera in the studio. [Shea] was the only stadium that had a studio. It was New York and something special. I was thrilled to be on his show."

Hernandez said Kiner was all business during his interview.

"It was very impersonal. Ralph was busy and he was doing his interview. He had his specific questions and it was very straightforward and business-like. There was no real great interaction other than me answering questions. He asked very pertinent baseball questions. He didn't ask stupid questions."

Hernandez had a burning desire to get on the show.

"Yes I did, which means I had to have a good day."

Getting on *Kiner's Korner* provided a lifelong memory for a kid who grew up on the West Coast.

"It was great to be on the show because I'd finally been on the Kiner show and I was 'star of the game.' That's always good. I was just too young, I was twenty-three years old so I was just thrilled to be on the show. I just know he asked pertinent questions about the game, he was a baseball guy. It was an easy interview."

You mentioned a $100 bill as your parting gift. Did Ralph hand you the money when you came in or when you got up to leave?

"He gave it to me right away. As soon as you sat down, when they were in commercial."

Your favorite moment of being on the show?

"The first time I was on, it was the most memorable for me because I finally got on the Ralph Kiner show."

Howard Johnson

Wednesday, July 29, 1987 @ Busch Stadium
Mets 6 Cardinals 4 (10 innings)

In December 1984, the New York Mets pulled off one of the best trades in their history when they dealt pitcher Walt Terrell to the Detroit Tigers in exchange for a switch-hitting, third baseman named Howard Johnson. During his nine year Mets career, "Ho Jo" displayed consistent power that included three seasons of 30 or more homeruns, while he stole over 20 bases in six straight seasons with a career high of 41 in 1989.

Johnson was part of a rare occurrence, as he appeared on *Kiner's Korner* after a road game. Most of the shows were broadcast from Shea Stadium but on this July night, "Ho Jo" was a road guest.

"I wasn't on a ton of them, but I was on enough. If I had to pick one, it would be on the field at Busch Stadium in '87. It was probably the most fun because usually when we did Kiner's Korner it was at home. We never really did it on the road, so when you got to do one on the road, it was cool and kind of special. Ralph did such a great job, everything was always positive, there

Howard Johnson: "I finally got on the Ralph Kiner show."
(Mark Rosenman)

was nothing negative. Even if you made a bad play, or struck out with the bases loaded, it wasn't like you would be on Kiner's Korner *and he would be grilling you about it. Nothing negative that would embarrass you, just pure positive Met stuff and the fans loved it. The show was so well thought of. Sure, Ralph would butcher names occasionally and at times it was funny to hear him do it, but at the end of the day the show was well thought of and Ralph was respected amongst the players."*

A guest spot on *Kiner's Korner* was highly sought after among the players.

"I wouldn't say it was a competition within the locker room, but it was always fun to be on Kiner's Korner. *Back then it was local and that's how you would get a lot of publicity. You would go on there and Ralph would talk to you after a good ballgame, so it was always something positive. Plus, the studio was just off the locker room so it was so convenient, which was a big plus. This way guys didn't mind having to go over there."*

Johnson said he would usually get the call to be on the show from a friendly face.

"The studio was right next door to the locker room so when you came up the tunnel at Shea from the dugout up through the walkway, the locker room would be right across the hall just to the right. The Kiner's Korner

studio was to the left of that, almost attached to the Jets' Locker room. So what would happen, the game would be over and Jay Horwitz [Mets Public Relations Director] would be there and tell you, 'Hey, Ralph wants you to be on the show.' You would go throw on a Mets pullover or something and head over to the show. It really was as quick as that. A lot of times you went on the show and the guys in the locker room didn't even know you were gone."

Johnson said the first time he saw the set, he was impressed.

"I just remember thinking how well it was being run. It all was just very cool. I walked in and there was Ralph at the desk. All the cameras were set up. Ralph pretty much got right to it. He told me what he was going to ask me, what clips he was going to show. It was so well done and the players appreciated it, because it was quick and easy. There wasn't a lot of work needed from the players end. They just put a mic on you and asked questions and it was just a really cool thing to be on as it had a real cult following in New York."

"HoJo" grew up in Florida and admitted he was not aware of the show or what Ralph accomplished on the field until he was dealt to New York.

"No, it was purely a Mets' production, it didn't seem to go outside of the New York Area. Once I arrived, guys talked about it in the clubhouse. Most of the times we would joke a bit about Ralph saying he was half drunk and getting names wrong. That was the main thing we joked about, but to a man everyone loved doing it, because he was so much fun to be around, and we had a deep appreciation for what he did."

"My perspective is that there was respect for Ralph, but as far as players being acutely aware of what he accomplished on the field, I don't think there was a real keen awareness of it. That is not a knock on me or any of my teammates, as that is still the way it is now a days. Players today are not privy to the stuff we did when we played. They may go back and Google or search you on the web, but back then you either knew it or you didn't. You couldn't do a search like you can today. We all knew that Ralph was a big-time player, but he never ever threw that at you during conversations to try and make himself look good. We all had respect for him though, and he had a mutual respect for us."

Ho Jo said the parting gift came in very handy.

I know I got a lot of watches, the good old Arbitron watch. I know I got an awful lot of those because we used to collect them and then use them as Christmas gifts to relatives. They were pretty cool. They had a Met logo and it was a nice watch."

Barry Lyons

Thursday, August 20ᵗ, 1987 @ Shea Stadium
Mets 7 Giants 4

Sunday, May 14, 1989 @ Shea Stadium (Mother's Day)
Mets 2 Padres 1

Barry Lyons was a major league catcher for seven years. Lyons played with the Mets in parts of seasons from 1986 through the first five months of the 1990 season, when he mainly served as Gary Carter's back up.

On August 20, 1987, Lyons's only career grand slam led the Mets past the Giants. It came in one of Lyons's rare starts but it landed him on *Kiner's Korner* as the star of the game

Barry Lyons—his Mother's Day appearance meant the world to him.
(Mark Rosenman)

Lyons was born in Biloxi, Mississippi, and did not know about the show until he got to New York.

"Down south, even today, we don't get SNY unless you have Direct TV with a special package, but back then my first year in the major leagues my friends and my family weren't really able to watch. After that first season I bought my mom and dad one of those big humungous satellite dishes for their backyard so they would be able to watch the games. I am a baseball lifer. I always had a passion for it, always studied the game from youth on up but unfortunately Ralph came along just a little before my time so I wasn't really aware of the show. Being blessed to be on the show a couple of times and then getting the opportunity to sit with Ralph at various Mets functions over the years and speak with him personally many times, I was really touched with him as a man, and a person. He was such a gentle soul and a kind gentleman. Over the years I learned of his greatness as a power-hitting player for the Pirates, a career that was pretty remarkable. It wasn't that lengthy compared to some of the great players but he was a special man that I didn't know a whole lot about before I had actually met him. Having met him and spent time with him, it was very clear, very evident what a good man he was."

Lyons was a rookie when he first came on the show and it turned into a memorable experience.

"It was impressive. I mean I was a young man from Biloxi, Mississippi, experiencing the bright lights of New York only a few times. As the Mets Minor League Player of the Year, they would bring you up to New York for a weekend in September and then I just got little doses of it as my career went on. So that was very special walking in there with all the lights and the set that was there with Ralph sitting in his customary spot. It truly was a very special feeling, a very warm and exciting feeling."

Kiner had a knack for making the guests feel comfortable and that included putting out a line or two that was not one of his famous "Kinerisms," but merely came from his vast knowledge of baseball history.

"It wasn't so much a 'Kinerism,' but the time I was on when I hit my grand slam, I was on with David Cone who had come on in relief and pitched a great game and got the win. Randy Myers got the save, but Ralph showed my grand slam and then his first comment after the replay was that now I only needed 22 more to catch Lou Gehrig."

Lyons was asked what kind of gift he received for being a guest of the show.

"An Armitron watch, a basic, no bells and whistles, nice watch. It didn't have a logo or a Kiner's Korner label or anything, just a nice little gift for being on."

Lyons's favorite moment on the show came in his second appearance.

"Just pouring my heart out to and wishing my mother a Happy Mother's day. Nothing can compare to that. My mother, father and brothers are so special to me, representing my family and being able to thank them, even though it was directed at my mother on Mother's Day. In reality it was to all of them for all they did to give me the opportunity to follow my dream."

Following the Mother's Day game, Lyons' second appearance came after he threw out three potential base stealers. Out of his two appearances, which one was his favorite.

"As amazing and awesome as it was to have hit a grand slam, being able to tell my Mother, Happy Mother's day and that the focus was on her, that has never been matched by anything else I have ever done in the game of baseball. To be able to honor my mother and to tell her on live television as she was sitting in the living room at her house "Happy Mother's day Mom, I love you, that was for you" I can't imagine a better gift for my mom. She means everything to me and my dad as well."

Ron Darling

Tuesday, April 12, 1988 @ Shea Stadium
Mets 3 Expos 0

In April 1982, the Mets traded popular outfielder Lee Mazzilli to the Texas Rangers for right-handed pitcher Walt Terrell and Ron Darling.

Terrell was eventually traded to the Detroit Tigers for Howard Johnson. Darling went on to be a solid pitcher for the Mets and was a big part of the 1986 World Series Championship team.

Darling went on to a career in broadcasting and is an analyst for Mets telecasts on SNY-TV. He also does games for TBS, including post-season.

Darling pitched a complete game, five-hit shutout in the home opener that netted him a spot on *Kiner's Korner* (see Chapter 7).

Ron Darling: "There was a 'grandfather' quality to him."
(Jeff Marquis, via Wikimedia Commons)

Darling said it was a thrill to go on a live show with Ralph Kiner.

"I didn't know what Kiner's Korner *was until I was asked to be on it. We didn't have TV's in the clubhouse. Bob Murphy was playing on the radio, no TV's were on so we never really watched* Kiner's Korner *but then you knew about it. Then you figured out two things, one, if you were asked to be on you were excited because you knew there was gonna be nothing but a ballplayer asking ballplayer questions. There was gonna be, not 'softball' would be the wrong choice, he was gonna ask you about the game. Literally have a question that pertained to baseball as opposed to something else. Also, you got, I think it was fifty dollars and then it went to a hundred dollars and it's before anyone knew what a 'benjamin' was. You just knew that it was a lot of money."*

Darling said Kiner had a trustful way about him.

"There was something about Ralph that, if he said, 'Hey listen, jump off this bridge,' you know it's probably not a good idea, but you trust him enough to do it. That's this 'grandfather' quality to him when we were playing that was just so sweet about him."

Darling said he was well versed on Kiner's place in baseball history.

"I grew up in a house where my parents loved baseball. We were given books on every great player to read. I knew more about Ralph Kiner than anyone should know at six, seven, eight years old. I remember one

thing I took from reading his biography is that he was from California. I had to find out what part of California because I'd never heard about it before. Alhambra, where's that? I know LA, I know San Francisco, where's Alhambra? I remember having to look it up. We had those encyclopedias in those days. His place in history has changed because of what has happened in the game. At that time, when I was six to ten years old, everyone knew who Ralph Kiner was because of where his place was on the list of home run hitters."

What was your initial impression of the set when you were on the show for the first time?

"It felt like we were doing the report from a janitor's closet. It didn't match the perfect jacket and tie that Ralph had on. The way he was as a man, so classy and it just felt like you were in a janitor's closet doing this thing. That maybe they had drawn it up about a second before he got in there. That wasn't so great but it's also the infancy of TV and post game things, people really didn't know what they were doing, although I don't know if so much has changed."

Do you remember anything about the set?

"It was a wood panel set and I was also on a set that was in the Jets clubhouse. I did one (show) where they just had a tiny sign, I know it's lost forever because I looked for it. They had a little sign to the left of Ralph and you did it, literally, sitting in the locker. If you knew the Jets locker in those days, there was kind of a mesh between each locker so if we had leaned back a little, it would've been like a confessional." (The sign does exist and is located in a sports bar in White Plains, New York)

Darling said he learned so much from working with Kiner as his partner on the broadcasts.

"I worked with Ralph. He being in the booth with me affects how I do a game. On a Thursday day game, twelve o'clock, he would be in at ten-thirty. I would make sure I got all my work done [by] ten-thirty so I could sit and talk to him about what he wanted to talk about that afternoon. It was the greatest kind of lessons that anyone could ever take. I always got more than I'm sure I gave to Ralph. It just was a delight. You know you've lived a good life, when you pass there is sadness and a smile would come to your face because he lived his life much better than any of us are gonna live ours."

Darling said whoever went on the show at that time, had to put up with the good natured ribbing they took from their teammates, not to mention "pony up" for some snacks and refreshments.

"A lot of guys would go 'What the f**k, you're on Kiner's Korner. 'What do you mean Kiner's Korner, I just threw a shutout.' So guys would kid each other, rib each other. At the end of it, people would go, 'Okay, you got the hundred bucks, you got the drinks tonight, or you got the chicken fingers or you got, whatever, potato skins. It became a real fanciful moment. You wanted to be on but if you didn't go on, you gave s**t to the person who's on"

"We're in St. Louis and Brent Gaff had been brought up. He was from nearby Indiana. Ralph was [describing how] a young pitcher for the Mets was making his debut, was gonna pitch for the Mets, was from nearby Indiana. He's got a lot of family members. 'Now pitching for the Mets, Brent Frank.' So Tim McCarver wrote down 'Gaff,' underlined it, and gave it to Ralph and Ralph looked at it and said, 'I am so sorry, I apologize.' Imagine getting it wrong, this young kid making his debut. 'Pitching for the Mets, Frank Gaff.'

Darling said Kiner never took himself seriously and that's what made him a good listener during his broadcasts.

"What Ralph did for Timmy is kinda what Keith does for me in that never forget that it's just a game. Never forgets that it should be entertaining. Timmy much like me, can get very serious about how we love to do the game but Ralph for Timmy and I know Keith for me. At some point we're watching baseball games and people are paying us. Let's not forget that. Ralph was about that. He loved the ballplayers, he loved the game, he respected it, and it came out in his voice. Class all the way."

Mackey Sasser

Friday, July 2, 1988 @ Shea Stadium (second game of a doubleheader)
Mets 5 Braves 1

Mackey Sasser played for the Mets for five seasons from 1988 to 1992. He was a career back up catcher who was known for his offense but had problems throwing the ball back to the pitcher that ultimately ended his career.

Mackey Sasser still has his parting gift, a leather jacket.
(Courtesy of Wendy Shotsky)

Sasser had two hits and two runs batted in to help the Mets increase their NL East lead over Pittsburgh to two games and he joined Ralph Kiner after the game.

"I hadn't heard about it when I was with the Giants or Pirates and maybe because I was only at Shea once. When I got to the Mets I found out about it from the guys on the team and what an honor it was to be on it. Usually when you got asked to go on that show, you had accomplished something pretty special that day and you had done something good for the team, so yeah it was something special to go on."

Sasser said that if you got the call, you were going on *Kiner's Korner*.

"Usually it was after a game, but on some occasions it was before a game. Jay Horwitz or an assistant would come get you in the locker room and tell you that they wanted you for Kiner's Korner. *Jay would let you know exactly when it was time to go. They would walk you down to the studio where they would wire you up with the microphones and then within minutes you were on the air talking about something you did in the game, or something that happened in the game or even about the next team coming in town. You really covered everything in a real short period of time."*

Sasser admitted having some butterflies when he went on the show.

"*The first time I ever really did any interviews was in New York. I tried not to be nervous or anything because they make you feel comfortable. You just go on and try and speak the best you can, but I was a little nervous when I walked in. It's only normal when you see the lights and the cameras. I still have nervous energy today when I do interviews on TV for the college team I coach, but once you get relaxed and get going before you know it you're done.*"

According to Sasser, there was universal respect for Kiner in the Mets clubhouse.

"*I can't speak for the other guys, but knew that his accomplishments were great, and some were trying to accomplish the same thing in the game. I don't think we ever talked about it in the clubhouse, but we all looked up to him. I know I did. I looked at what he did and knew I was never going to do that. I was just a scrappy player, but you look at what he accomplished and it's amazing. My office at the college has photos of mostly every first pitch I ever caught. There are movie stars, athletes, and one with Ralph Kiner. I've got all of them on my wall and to me it means a lot more because I met these people. Mickey Mantle, Ralph, those guys did the game right and I was part of that game. It makes me feel good that I can sit back and look at a picture and have it bring back the memories and good feelings*"

Sasser was honored to have inspired a Kinerism.

"*Ralph called me 'Mickey' all the time, but I knew what he meant, but that's what made him special. Ralph was such a great guy he knew the game, I look back on that now and I only wish I could have done it more. He made me something because when I was on that show people listened to me and my name got out there even if it was Mickey. I surely wasn't the only one he messed up. He messed up names the latter part of his career. He called me Mickey three years ago when I was at a banquet. He was in a wheelchair and it was the first time I had seen him in a long time and he called me Mickey. Did that offend me no! It actually made me smile.*"

Sasser noted Ralph Kiner was unique as a broadcaster because of the way he related to all the players.

"*To me Ralph respected the athlete. He understood the people that were around him. Today the media is always looking for something. Ralph was never ever looking for something, he was looking to interview you, make you feel comfortable, do what he needed to do and get you out of there. Today the interviewers are always searching for something, any little thing that went wrong and that is the major difference between media today and the way Ralph was. Ralph was always about the good part of the game. It was about the good plays the good accomplishments of your team and he knew how to ask the questions because he was an athlete. He was relaxed in his own body and made you feel the same way."*

The nine-year major leaguer appreciated one gift in particular for appearing on the show.

"Some of the things I got were a watch, some gift certificates but my favorite was a leather jacket. I still actually have it and I wore it awhile back. Everyone was asking where did you get that thing. I also got some shirts, but the leather jacket was my favorite."

Being on the show was something that Sasser would never forget.

"It meant I did something good for the New York Mets. I accomplished a goal that day and that was the reason I was on the show."

John Franco

Thursday, April 19, 1990 @ Shea Stadium
Mets 4 Cubs 1

Pitcher John Franco played twenty-one seasons in the major leagues where he posted 424 career saves, the most in baseball history by a left-hander. Franco is a native New Yorker who played his high school ball at Lafayette High in Brooklyn and college ball at St. John's University.

He began his career with the Cincinnati Reds but in the winter of 1989, he was traded to the Mets, the team he grew up rooting for.

The lefthander was a guest of *Kiner's Korner* as both a Red and a Met.

"When I was a kid growing up, I always used to watch Kiner's Korner. *After the ballgames, I'd want to see what guest he had on, whether it would be from the Mets or a visiting team player. I found it interesting. Always hoped to have the home team on but, unfortunately, it didn't always work out that way."*

Who was the person who directed you to be on?

"Probably Jay Horwitz would be the guy. I don't remember anybody specific, but if it was anybody, it was probably Jay Horwitz."

John Franco: "You have to pinch yourself that you are in that seat where some great players were there before you."

(Mark Rosenman)

What were your impressions of the studio after having watched it on TV as a kid?

"The studio wasn't too far from the locker room. It sure was different from today's studios, that's for sure. It was a little room with some light, some chairs, a couple of cameras in there, Ralph's seat and the player's seat."

Ralph was not known as a polished broadcaster. What did you think of his interviewing skills.

"He was right to the point. Whatever point of the game that he was trying to make, he would come to you and ask you a question about a certain pitch that you made in a certain situation. Talked about growing up in Brooklyn, being a Met fan stuff like that. Just like any other reporter. The only thing is he was an ex-player."

Franco said Ralph Kiner commanded respect.

"I just thought he was one of the top players in the game back in his time. I just thought he was real gentleman. Got right to the point and you had that respect for a Hall of Famer who was interviewing you. You want to give him all the respect that you can."

Were you awestruck by meeting those people he saw on TV as a youngster.

"As a kid growing up you want to play for the team that you rooted for which I was fortunate enough to do for the Mets. You just want to do everything that you've seen as a kid. Meet Ralph Kiner, meet Bob Murphy, grow vegetables in the bullpen like Joe Pignatano. It was like living out a dream. When you see these things as a kid, you kinda have to pinch yourself that you are in that seat where some great players were there before you."

What parting gift did you get from being on the show?

"I think it was a fifty dollar certificate for 'The Wiz' or something. When guys would be on the show, they would give the gift certificate to the clubhouse guys."

6

"Jamie Lee Curtis throws her arms around Kiner and says, 'Daddy!'"

WHEN RALPH KINER and Tim McCarver were broadcasting a game in Philadelphia a number of years ago, a famous actress prompted a memorable encounter.

Actress Jamie Lee Curtis and her husband Christopher Guest were walking through the press box that day. Kiner wanted to meet Jamie Lee Curtis because he had dated her mother, Janet Leigh.

Kiner approached the actress and said, "Jamie Lee, my name's Ralph Kiner. I wanted to tell you that I used to date your mother." At that moment, Jamie Lee Curtis throws her arms around Kiner and says, "Daddy, I've finally found you!"

"Chris Wheeler [the Phillies announcer] is a good friend of mine and is a good friend of Christopher Guest," McCarver said, "and he knew both of them very well. They were huge Phillies fans. Ralph loved to tell that story because it made him younger. Telling a story like that makes you younger. When a good-looking woman throws her arms around you and kiddingly says 'Daddy,' well, that makes you feel good."

Jamie Leigh Curtis, right, with her mother, Janet Leigh
(Alan Light, via Wikimedia Commons)

"The score is the New York Giants, who moved to San Francisco, two, and the Mets, one."

Phil Mushnick pens the column "Equal Time" for the *New York Post* and has reported on New York sports media for over four decades.

Mushnick said Kiner's game recaps were legendary:

"This was 1986, in the wrap up with Steve Zabriske. It was a game in Houston that was televised on Channel 9. This is him [Kiner] explaining why Jesse Orosco didn't get the save: 'He did not have, he did not pitch three innings and he came in with, ah, out the, ah, the on-deck batter being a batter that he would face in, ah, his next approach to pitching to the hitter.'"

Mushnick once asked the kind-hearted and generous Kiner to help him out with a charity event:

"I thought he knew me. He did know me. He knew my name, he said he read my stuff, either way it was okay. I called him and I said 'Listen, any shot you can [donate a signed ball for charity]?' We had a charity golf outing and he [Kiner] was a golfer and he said 'Yeah, give me your address, I'll send you

an autographed baseball' which we auctioned. How it got to my house, I'll be damned. I lived on 28 Corona Court, Old Bridge, New Jersey. The package was sent to 'Farrel Muchinick, 28 Corona Court, All Brige, NY,' but he got the zip code right which is how I got it."

David J. Halberstam is the author of *Sports on New York Radio: A Play-By-Play History*. When Kiner died in 2014, Mushnick recalled that Halberstam had sent him two of his fondest Kiner memories.

"[Kiner] caught himself in mid-sentence calling the San Francisco Giants the New York Giants. Improvising as only Ralph could, he said, 'The score is the New York Giants, who moved to San Francisco, two, and the Mets, one.'"

"The other one was when announcers were kept abreast of out of town scores by ticker tape. Paper shreds collected under their chairs. Ralph at the time was an inveterate cigar smoker. One day the ticker tape caught fire after enough of Ralph's cigar ashes collected on the heap of ticker tape."

7

"Well, Mayor, congratulations and I'm glad you're a part of this."

OLD EPISODES OF *Kiner's Korner* are practically nowhere to be found but we uncovered some that are transcribed in this chapter.

September 17, 1986
Mets 4 Cubs 2

After the Mets clinched the 1986 National League Eastern Division title, WOR TV aired a special edition of *Kiner's Korner* that featured player interviews from a raucous Mets clubhouse. In the beginning of the show, Kiner, who was right outside the clubhouse, is seen interviewing the VIP's who were in attendance at Shea Stadium.

Kiner had never won anything as a player but 1986 would be the third time that he was able to broadcast and be a small part of a victorious locker room.

Ralph: "Well we have the number one citizen of New York City, the Mayor, Mayor Ed Koch, and Mayor, congratulations on bringing a team in here that has won the Eastern division championship."

Mayor Ed Koch: "Well, I was talking with the owners tonight and they said six years ago, there were 1300 people and that included the ushers in this Stadium. Tonight there were about 50,000. The electricity was extraordinary."

Ralph: "You've been out here and you've often thrown out the first ball many times. Back in 1969 when Mayor [John] Lindsay was the mayor of New York City, he really got elected on the victory of the New York Mets."

Koch: "That is true. I'm not running this year. I'm here because I love the team."

Ralph: "Well, the team certainly coming through here and winning and I'm glad they could do it here in New York despite of the fact it might be a disaster for your stadium."

Koch: "We're gonna have a ticker tape parade when they win the World Series."

Ralph: "Well, Mayor, congratulations and I'm glad you're a part of this."

Koch: "Thank you very much."

After Tim McCarver was soaked with champagne in the clubhouse, he "threw" it to Kiner who was outside the clubhouse with General Manager Frank Cashen. Kiner's ability to ad-lib was on full display as he began the interview.

Ralph: "Well, so far it's dry over here in this corner, *Kiner's Korner,* and we have with us, the architect of this great ball club and it is Frank Cashen who put together the organization that has brought this championship to New York City, and Frank I guess congratulations certainly are in order and I know that you've experienced this before in Baltimore but I wonder if this is as big a thrill as it was in Baltimore."

GM Frank Cashen: "Well it is and I'm especially happy for the owners, Mr. Doubleday and Mr. Wilpon who stood behind us while we built this ballclub and it took a little time, took some of their money and they were very patient and they deserve a lot of the credit."

Eventually, Kiner moved into the clubhouse where the celebration was really going strong as he prepared to interview Keith Hernandez.

Ralph: "Well, back here in the clubhouse of the New York Mets, it's bedlam as you can see. The champagne being poured around, squirted around, what have you and I have Keith Hernandez who certainly will be considered the most valuable player on this ball club and Keith, you came into the ballgame today a little under the weather with a cold or a flu, whatever it was, you did get in at the last, you wanted to do that.

(Hernandez did not start the game but came in as a defensive replacement for Dave Magadan in the eighth inning)

Keith Hernandez: "I told Davey [Mets manager Davey Johnson] that uhh . . ."

At that point, Hernandez who was under the weather, had a full ice bucket poured on him by Mets relief pitcher Roger McDowell.

Hernandez: "That's gonna be great for my flu."

Kiner concluded the interview in his own imitable style.

Ralph: "One thing about being up here with that ice thrown all over you, you will get rid of your cold and you'll get pneumonia and you can cure that. Keith Hernandez and we'll return right after this message from 'Mit-Su-Bih-shee (instead of "Mit-su-bee-shee) Motors."

Kiner went on to interview some of the other players including third-baseman Ray Knight

Ralph: "Well our guest right here Ray Knight and the Mets would not be in the position they're in right now but Ray coming up with a great year after not having that kind of a year the year before."

Kiner was not immune to getting soaked as part of the celebratory atmosphere. As the announcer is closing the show by reading the sponsors, there is a shot of Kiner who is covered with shaving cream and champagne.

September 12, 1987
Mets 4 Expos 2

Mets reliever Roger McDowell, who was known as a prankster, was always an interesting guest on *Kiner's Korner*.

After saving the Mets 4–2 win over the Montreal Expos with an inning and two thirds of scoreless relief, he and second-baseman Wally Backman sat down with Ralph on the show. Kiner did not pass up the opportunity to banter with the outgoing McDowell.

Ralph: "Well, our guest on the show here, Roger McDowell. Roger is that the basic dress for a relief pitcher day."

(McDowell was wearing his warmup jacket with a towel wrapped around his neck)

Roger McDowell: "After throwing a hard inning and two thirds, this is the way you dress."

McDowell was well known for giving teammates "hotfoots" in the dugout. Kiner seized the opportunity to bring up his propensity for practical jokes.

Ralph: "I have a question that I have for you. The other day they had 'Smokey the Bear' out here and it was Fire Prevention Week or month, whatever, and of all people to accept the award, you start more fires than anybody I've ever seen. You put out a few too, though."

McDowell: "There's a basic premise, for every fire you put out the fire so 'Smokey' is the guy that I go to whenever I do a 'hotfoot' or anything like that."

Ralph: "'Cause everytime you look down that dugout, there is a fire going on."

McDowell: "Yeah, there's been a few times when the camera's caught it but we always "forewarned" Bill Webb (director) when it's gonna happen."

During the scoreboard portion of the show, Kiner called Chicago Cubs losing pitcher and former Met Ed Lynch, "Ed Leach." While reading the score of the Texas Rangers – Milwaukee Brewers game, Kiner noted that Paul Molitor extended his hitting streak to twenty-seven games by saying, "Good job, Paul Millitor."

April 14, 1986
Cardinals 6 Mets 2

Continuing a long tradition of booking future Hall of Famers, Kiner asked the acrobatic Cardinals shortstop Ozzie Smith to appear on *Kiner's Korner*.

Ralph: "The Cardinals told you not to do that back flip that you always did for special occasions. What happened there?

Ozzie Smith: "With the type of flip that it was, I put a lot of strain on the particular area [rotator cuff] that I hurt. They felt in the best interests of everybody concerned, I did not do it. So I had my son do it."

Ralph: "You did have a designated 'back-flipper.'?"

Smith: "He's the designated 'back-flipper'. I thought he was gonna back out on me but he took it. He went out and said 'hey, I'm gonna do it.' He's three years old and it was a fun evening. People enjoyed it."

August 25, 1985
Mets 9 Padres 3

Dwight Gooden won his twentieth game as the Mets beat the Padres. Darryl Strawberry homered.. After the game, Kiner had both of the Mets' exciting young players on the show. Strawberry had played despite dealing with injured fingers that he got while sliding into first base.

Darryl Strawberry: "I gotta kinda back off slidin' into first and try to go back to my usual slide and stay in the lineup.
Ralph: "I think that would be very wise because those fingers are very important to hitting."
Ralph: "So Dwight, a big event in your life and of course you've been going along now here in your second year coming up with new records as you go along and of course that one a big one. Youngest player to ever win twenty games in the major leagues. One of the things that's interesting, you were 17–9 last year, 20–3 this year. That totals up to an awful lot of wins and a great percentage."
Dwight Gooden: "Yeah, it's just a great honor to have."

April 12, 1988
Mets 3 Expos 0

Ron Darling goes the distance to shut out Montreal in the 1988 home opener. After the game, Darling went the distance from the clubhouse to the *Kiner's Korner* studio.

Darling appeared on set with an ice pack on his shoulder after winning the game

Ralph: "Ron, people are looking at you right now of course and they're wondering what all that is that you have on and maybe you can explain it. I know you can do it better than I."

Ron Darling: "I guess a doctor would explain it. You break blood vessels when you pitch and they expand and swell and the way to take down that swelling is with ice. Hurt my back a little in the second inning so that's why I got something on my rib cage here, sort of look like the Elephant Man here."

Ralph (laughs); "You really do."

Kiner was an outfielder during his playing career but his line of questioning for Darling really brought his knowledge of the game to the forefront. Kiner began with a technical question based on the weather conditions which were cold and windy.

Ralph: "You change anything when it is cold like that because it is hard to grip the ball, you don't have that feel."

Darling: "My big pitch is my split finger and it isn't really a good pitch for me until the real hot weather where I can really grip the ball. In the cold weather, I really change it. I make the grip a little closer so I'm almost throwing a fastball but just take a little off, but for me to throw a real wide split fingered fastball, I'd never throw it for a strike."

8

"Well, you're not going to root for the Yankees and the Giants are gone, they are the best National League team in town."

GARY DELL'ABATE, AKA "Baba Booey," is the executive producer and has worked on the "The Howard Stern Show" since 1984. Dell'Abate grew up in Long Island and is an avid Mets fan. In May of 2009, Dell'Abate threw out the ceremonial first pitch at a Mets game. It was labeled "the most embarrassing ceremonial first pitch in baseball history." The ball landed down the third base line and hit an umpire. [2]

Dell'Abate has fond memories of *Kiner's Korner*.

"My dad would be watching it. I remember being a little kid and always watching Mets' games but the game wasn't over because there was Kiner's Korner. *As a little kid, I was like 'well why is he watching this guy talk because the game is over.'"*

Your passion for the Mets comes from your dad?

"It is completely and utterly from my dad. My dad was a die-hard Dodgers fan. He probably cried with half of New York when they left. When the National League team came in [the Mets in 1962] that was his team. For a lot of people it was like, 'Well, you're not going to root for the Yankees and the Giants are gone, they are the best National League team in town. It didn't matter how bad they were, they're our team."

So that was the bond you shared watching the games and *Kiner's Korner*.

"Yeah, and as I got older I would kind of goof about it like 'Oh, he's still on.' It was like comfort food and it was interesting. Even years later, my dad moved down to Florida, and I'd call him and ask if he saw the Met game and then we would talk about the game."

Do you have any recollections of some of your favorite players that were on the show?

"I would say 1968–69, when they won the World Series, was the first year I seriously watched baseball because I was only eight. I remember [Tom] Seaver was my favorite player. [Ron] Swoboda, guys like that. Seaver seemed to be on there like he belonged on there. Swoboda seemed to be happy he was invited."

Favorite Met moment?

"It's not even up for discussion. It's the '86 Mets. My dad and I were at Game Six. It was insanity. You went from thinking that a team that had led wire to wire was about to blow a World Series to, 'We're back and we can still play and win this.' It was unbelievable."

How much baseball history do you think you absorbed from watching *Kiner's Korner* and the games themselves with Bob Murphy, Lindsey Nelson, and Kiner?

"You learned a lot because they would talk about players. They would talk about Jackie Robinson of course but then they would talk about players like Carl Erskine and Roy Campanella. Those three announcers were the best. Kiner, Murphy, and Nelson were just such a part of my childhood. I thought they were all amazing."

You're a person who works in the media and has watched Howard Stern conduct interviews on a daily basis. When you reflect on *Kiner's Korner*, does working in the business make you appreciate the show more?

"The show had little production value. You could practically see the set swaying, so it wasn't difficult to produce. It was Kiner speaking to the 'star of the game' for fifteen minutes and Kiner was really good at that. That was his forte. Talking to people."

Why is there such a fondness for Ralph Kiner?

"He was a Hall of Famer that belonged to the Mets. He wasn't a Mets player so he had credibility. It seems goofy now, but Kiner was on for so long, we

remember him as the 'old guy.' It was probably a big deal to be on the show with a Hall of Famer."

If you were to try and explain what *Kiner's Korner* was to someone who had never seen it, how would you describe it?

"It was a short show after the baseball game where the Mets announcer talked to the 'star of the game' for fifteen minutes and chats with him about what happened in the game. Sometimes it would go into any area they were interested in talking about that day. It was a man's man talking baseball with a baseball player."

Rock and Roll Legend

George Thorogood and the Delaware Destroyers have been entertaining rock and roll fans for more than forty years. The band has produced some classic hits like "Bad to the Bone," "Who Do You Love?", "Move it on Over," and "One Bourbon, One Scotch, One Beer."

Thorogood is an avid baseball fan. In 1976, he played second base on a semi-pro team that was part of the Roberto Clemente League but the rocker decided music was a better option than baseball.

Thorogood grew up in Delaware, but eventually became a fan of the New York Mets.

How did you become a Mets fan?

"At the time I was reading a lot about the New York Giants. The Phillies broke my heart in '64 so I didn't want anything to do with them anymore. I just started reading up about it. The Mets are a good team for me because they never win. The Phillies never won either, they were perennial losers. When they got real close to the pennant and they lost, I said, 'I don't want to do that anymore' so I'm gonna pick somebody that always loses so I won't have to go through this again.' They they (the Mets) put me through it again. Then they went and won the World Series in '69 and went and blew their image."

Thorogood said baseball on television wasn't as prevalent as it is today. *"Back in those days it's not like now. Baseball is on 24 hours a day. Every team is on television. Back in the '60's and '70's there was hardly anything on television about baseball."*

Thorogood is well versed in baseball history and he knew the origin of the title, *Kiner's Korner*.

"He got that name, Kiner's Korner, when he played in Pittsburgh because he hit the ball over the left field fence at Forbes Field. That was known as Kiner's Korner."

The show was simple, but it worked.

"I didn't know there was a Kiner's Korner until probably the '80's. A couple of times I watched it. I met him once, met him in Pittsburgh. The show was like five minutes long. It was just him interviewing the guy who just hit a sacrifice fly and won the game. If nothing was happening, he'd interview Tom Seaver. It was okay."

Even with his busy schedule, Thorogood finds time to follow the Mets.

"When I'm on the road, I turn on the TV and watch them. If they win I buy the paper the next day. If they don't win, I don't buy the paper."

Thorogood put his passion for the Mets in perspective.

"Always follow a loser. You always get a good seat at the park. The Yankees finish second, you think you'd had a terrible year. The Mets finish third, you'd had a good year."

Acting Like a Fan

Charles Grodin is an award winning actor and a well known Met fan, who has appeared in such films as *Midnight Run*, *The Heartbreak Kid*, *Heaven Can Wait*, and *Catch-22*.

In 1986, the Mets were playing the Houston Astros in the National League Championship Series. The series took place while Grodin was shooting scenes for the CBS mini-series *Fresno*.

In order to follow his beloved Mets, a large screen TV that was tuned to the game was set up right outside of camera range on Stage 4 at the Studio Center in Los Angeles.[3]

Grodin said he became a Met fan because "it was the time when [George] Steinbrenner was hiring and firing Billy Martin, and I was just looking for something relaxing."

Grodin's first exposure to Ralph Kiner was when he was growing up in Pittsburgh, Pennsylvania.

"When I was a young boy in Pittsburgh going to the Pirate games," Grodin said during a recent interview, *"we never went home until Ralph Kiner had his last at bat. My most vivid memory of Ralph as a person is*

when I was sitting with him in the broadcast booth during the Met game and he quoted a line from a book I had just written. It was, "Don't ever yell at anyone, they'll hate you forever."

Mets radio play-by-play announcer

Howie Rose is living a dream as the Mets radio play-by-play broadcaster. Rose began broadcasting Mets games on television but eventually moved over to radio fulltime.

The Queens, New York, native spent his childhood in the shadow of Shea Stadium and is considered a Mets historian.

"My default memory is 1969 and one game down the stretch Cleon [Jones] and [Tommie] Agee were on and they were talking about the comeback", Rose said. I just remember when Cleon patted Agee on the thigh and said, 'With my man here, there is nothing we can't do' or something like that and I was struck with the love those guys had as teammates and it was so deep because they grew up together."

Rose recalled how he was so impressed with a guest from the opposition

"Another one I remember is after [Pirates pitcher] Bob Moose pitched a no hitter and it was four days before they clinched first place in the division. For a fifteen-year old who was very, very, very wrapped up in the whole thing, I never assumed they were going to win the World Series until the ball landed in Cleon's glove. Even four days away from first place I wasn't taking anything for granted. I think they lost Friday and Saturday and I was thinking, "Oh please, no." Sunday they had a double header. They won the first game, and between games Ralph had [Pirates broadcasters] Bob Prince in the studio for a Kiner's Korner. Prince talked about the Mets so reverentially by saying, 'You're going to win this'. It was funny to me that someone on the other team would accept the inevitability that the Mets would win the division title. So it didn't have anything to do with Ralph."

As a kid, the Queens native said there was always a need for information.

"Oh yeah. I heard that young fans are as inquisitive today as our generation certainly was," Rose said. "I just read voraciously about the game. When a player entered my consciousness, I'd go read about him however I could. There were books and encyclopedias, my dad was a great resource and other

baseball fans were a great resource. And I'd just ask questions and I don't know if kids do that anymore, they got more resources than we ever did. But I went to school on guys like Ralph; you don't have to be a scholar to look at Ralph and what he did in a short amount of time and say, "Wow, that's a career."

Rose can remember a very special edition of *Kiner's Korner*.

"My favorite episode is when Ralph had me on as a guest, which I think I wrote about in my book. I'll never forget when he said, "Come to think of it, you're the worst guest we've ever had," and I can hear the howl from the control rooms. That was memorable to hear the music and see the set," said Rose.

TV play-by-play announcer for NBA basketball

Mike Breen is the TV voice of the New York Knicks on MSG Television and ABC/ESPN's coverage of NBA basketball. Breen set a record for TV play-by-play announcers by calling his tenth NBA Finals in June of 2015. The Fordham graduate grew up in Yonkers, New York, and is a long time, die hard Mets fan.

Breen said part of the charm of watching *Kiner's Korner* was seeing the out-of-town stars.

"You never got a chance to hear these guys talk back in those days, especially the visiting players," Breen said. A guy like Tom Seaver, you knew what he sounded like when he spoke, but so many of the visiting players. A guy like Pete Rose, or Roberto Clemente, or even Keith Hernandez. Those guys, like you never heard them speak. They really humanized baseball players back then when nobody was doing that."

Breen said a show like *Kiner's Korner* would be hard to do in today's broadcasting of sporting events.

"Today, it's hard to get the players to do that, especially star players. The only way you get it now," Breen said, "for example, the NBA when they're just walking off the court and before they go to the locker room. Back then it was like an honor. The players seemed to be so grateful to be asked to have Ralph Kiner ask them to be on his show. What always struck me was the respect that they showed him. They knew that this guy wasn't just a former major league player, he was a great player. To me that always came across on how respectful they were to him."

Breen, who's conducted numerous interviews, said Kiner was under-rated as an interviewer.

"You pray that you've got somebody [on as a guest] who's got the 'gift of the gab.' If it was a talkative person he [Kiner] just sat back and let him talk and if it was one of those that was a man of few words, he would fill in all the blanks. He seemed to have a way of making the guests very comfortable, even though he never really seemed completely comfortable being on camera himself."

Breen said *Kiner's Korner* inspired him when he became a broadcaster.

"He would have two guys on at a time quite a bit and I don't remember that being done. When we sit down to do our interviews for ESPN, it's almost 99 percent of the time we sit down and we talk to one guy. Every once in a while, because one guy is an introvert, I'll ask for a second guy. He might have a good relationship with that guest or if we hear about two teammates that are really close, we'll have them sit down because they're so much more comfortable if they're not alone being interviewed. Maybe that's why he [Kiner] did it. Back then to have two major leaguers interact, it was thrilling for a kid to watch something like that."

Ralph was known for his 'malaprops.' How do you think those would go over on today's broadcasts?

Author Mark Rosenman's moment on the *Korner*.
(Mark Rosenman)

"I think the scrutiny today sometimes gets a little over the top because anybody who's ever done live television, if you're on long enough, you're gonna say some silly things and we've all said many silly things because it's live television and that's what makes it so much fun. As much as we like to make fun of the malaprops, his knowledge of the game was just phenomenal and he did have great recall."

POSTSCRIPT

AS WE WERE wrapping up this book, the 2015 New York Mets were making a surprising run to the National League pennant and a trip to the World Series.

It was the fifth National League championship in Mets' history. The show, *Kiner's Korner*, was there for the previous four so a thought came to mind.

What guests would Ralph have had on the show during the 2015 season?

After earning his first major league win, Kiner would have wanted Steven Matz as his guest. How many times would Ralph, in his lovable and inimitable manner, call Steven Matz, "Steven Mets"?

Kiner would be thrilled to have Jacob deGrom, Matt Harvey, and Noah Syndergaard on the show because he had a great appreciation for talent. You can bet Ralph would provide the fans with something to remember from at least two of those three names.

Kirk Nieuwenhuis would be sitting next to Ralph after he had his memorable three-home run game. Kiner's attempt to pronounce Nieuwenhuis would have provided some wonderful memories.

How about Wilmer Flores sitting down with Ralph after he cried because he thought he was traded?

Giants' pitcher Chris Heston would've joined *Kiner's Korner* after he pitched his no-hitter against the Mets at CitiField. You could smile with certainty that, sometime during the show, Ralph would identify Chris Heston as "Charlton Heston."

Following the four-game sweep of the Cubs in the National League Championship Series, there would have been a special episode of *Kiner's Korner*. As was the case in the previous four pennant celebrations, Ralph would be there conducting his interviews with players and executives and wearing a towel around his neck to help limit the soaking that he took while the champagne flowed.

Kiner loved every minute of those raucous celebrations.

Just as the millions of his fans, young and old, loved every minute of *Kiner's Korner*.

ACKNOWLEDGMENTS

Mark Rosenman

First and foremost I want to acknowledge my amazing wife Beth who is an endless source of encouragement and support. I also want to thank my children, Josh and Liana, who by the way they approach everything they do with such passion inspires me to do the same.

I am grateful to my late father Morris who after working hard all day always found the time to take me to Mets games. I was lucky enough to see both Mets' World championships with him. Also, my mother Estelle allowed me to buy every sports book whenever there was a book fair at school and still encourages me to pursue my passions. My sister Cheryl and my late sister Suzie always set great examples for their little brother.

My best friend Jeff Cohen who no doubt watched more Kiner's Korners and went to more Met games with me then anyone else in the world and still is my favorite person in the world to talk sports with.

I would like to thank the following members of the press who welcomed me into the Citifield press box with open arms and showed me the ropes including Kenny Albert, Larry Brooks, Gary Cohen, Ed Coleman, Steve Gelbs, Kevin Kernan, David Lennon, Josh Lewin, Marty Noble, Howie Rose, and Adam Rubin.

Thank you to The New York Mets PR department, in particular Jay Horwitz, who helped me in gaining access to the players during their busiest time of year.

Thank you to the WLIE SportstalkNy interns Liam Beatus, Jake Lampert, and Matt Weinstein who were a huge help in transcribing hours and hours of interviews.

Phil Gries of Archival Television Audio Inc. and Joe Barbarisi of Phenia Films who shared their copies of vintage *Kiner's Korners* with us.

A note of thanks to my WLIE 540am *SPORTSTALKNY* show family, AJ Carter, my co-host, our sponsors Leith Baren, Neil Cohen, Gary Pincus, Andrew and David Reale, and Rob Solomon. Your support of the show is the reason this book is even possible. The hundreds of authors who have appeared on "WLIE 540am *SPORTSTALKNY*" who have inspired me over the years.

Thanks to the staff at Skyhorse Publishing, in particular Niels Aaboe who gave a rookie a shot.

Last but not least my writing partner in this project, Howie Karpin, who just as Tim McCarver brought out the best in Ralph Kiner, pushes me to be my best.

Howie Karpin

So many to thank but I must start with my immediate family: My lovely wife Kathy, and my two boys, Danny, and Jake Karpin; my sister and her husband, Carol and Barry Shore; my nieces, Wendy Rosano Shore, Sharon Shore and their families.

Gary Axelbank, Jay Brustman, Gary Cohen, Rich Coutinho, Mark Feinman (who helped inspire this book), Mike Mancuso, Steve Marcus, Wallace Matthews, Jay Nadler, Lew Rose, Gary Simon, Jordan Sprechman and David Wright.

My Elias buddies, Bob Waterman and John Labombarda

My Edgemont and Croes softball friends

And all the friends (and I have been blessed with many) that have been a part of my life throughout the years.